Essential
Moscow and Leningrad

by

CHRISTOPHER AND MELANIE RICE

Christopher Rice writes regularly on Russian and Soviet affairs and holds a PhD from the Centre for Russian and East European Studies at Birmingham University. His wife Melanie is also a writer and has shared his fascination with Moscow and Leningrad ever since their first joint visit in 1978.

AA

Produced by the Publishing Division of
The Automobile Association

Written by Christopher and Melanie Rice
Peace and Quiet section by Paul Sterry
Consultant: Frank Dawes

Edited, designed and produced by the Publishing Division of The Automobile Association. Maps © The Automobile Association 1991

Distributed in the United Kingdom by the Publishing Division of The Automobile Association, Fanum House, Basingstoke, Hampshire, RG21 2EA

The contents of this publication are believed correct at the time of printing. Nevertheless, the publishers cannot accept responsibility for errors or omissions, nor for changes in details given. We have tried to ensure accuracy in this guide, but things do change and we would be grateful if readers could advise us of any inaccuracies they may encounter.

A CIP catalogue record for this book is available from the British Library.

ISBN 0 7495 0088 3

Published by The Automobile Association

Typesetting: Tradespools Ltd, Frome, Somerset

Colour separation: B.T.B. Reprographics, Whitchurch, Hampshire

Printed in Italy by Printers SRL, Trento

Front cover picture: St Basil's Cathedral

This book employs a
simple rating system to
help choose which
places to visit:

     do not miss

     see if you can

     worth seeing if
you have time

A Superpower's capital and a prime tourist attraction: Moscow

INTRODUCTION

We still call it Russia, but officially it is the Union of Soviet Socialist Republics (USSR). The largest country in the world, stretching nearly 9,000 miles (15,000km) from east to west, the USSR covers nearly one-sixth of the earth's surface, and is more than 90 times bigger than Great Britain. Russia, now called the Russian Federation, is actually just one (albeit the largest) of 15 republics, each with its own history, culture, language and traditions. The capital of the USSR and of the Russian Federation is Moscow. With a population of 8.7 million, Moscow is not only the largest city in the Soviet Union, but also one of the great capitals of Europe and a thriving commercial, industrial and communications centre. Leningrad, with more than 4 million inhabitants, is the USSR's second city. For more than 200 years, from 1703 to 1918, it was the capital, first as St Petersburg,

then, during the First World War, as Petrograd.
Finally, after the death of Lenin in 1924, it was
renamed Leningrad. It remains an important
seaport and industrial centre, but visitors are
attracted to it for its rich architectural and artistic
heritage and its vibrant cultural life. For sheer
beauty Leningrad has few equals.

Moscow, Russia's Soul

Think of the Soviet Union and the chances are
you think of the Kremlin with its great fortress
walls, gleaming cupolas and ornate palaces. For
centuries this was a place of refuge, from the
ravages of cruel Tatar hordes, from the excesses
of tyrannical serf-owners, from the spectre of
poverty and hunger. Today it is the seat of
government of one of the world's most powerful
states, as well as the country's premier tourist
attraction. Beyond the Kremlin is a city full of
architectural monuments and fascinating places
of interest: Red Square—the garish St Basil's
Cathedral contrasting with the sombre Lenin
mausoleum; the elegant Bolshoi Theatre;
charming Arbat, with its street musicians and
pavement artists; the Tretyakov Gallery,
overflowing with artistic treasures. You can shop
on the fashionable Gorky Street or in the GUM
department store; explore the luxurious and
amazingly efficient metro system; travel back in
time by visiting some of the city's ancient
churches and monasteries, many restored for
worship. You can attend a rock concert in Gorky
Park, watch a football match, or take a stroll
through the Exhibition of Economic
Achievements. You can eat in any number of the
city's loud and colourful ethnic restaurants, or
take a night out at the world famous State Circus.
Whatever your taste, there is something in
Moscow for you.

Leningrad, Window on the West

Leningrad is an artificial creation, the brainchild
of one man: the modernising tsar, Peter the
Great. Turning his back on Moscow, which he
despised as primitive and backward-looking,
Peter chose a site on the shores of the Baltic and
transformed an unpromising landscape of
islands and marshland into one of the world's
most beautiful cities. He called it St Petersburg.
Now, nearly 300 years later, Leningrad is a

INTRODUCTION

*Buskers in Arbat
Street, Moscow, a
magnet for artists,
poets and musicians*

thriving metropolis; but it is also a unique
architectural monument—a dazzling ensemble
of palaces and cathedrals, rivers and canals,
grandiose squares and sweeping perspectives,
a succession of beautiful pinks, greens, blues
and yellows.

For the art lover, Leningrad, with its 50 museums
and art galleries, is a paradise. The Hermitage
alone boasts works by Raphael and da Vinci,
Rembrandt and Rubens, Cézanne and van Gogh,
Picasso and Matisse. Or, if your interests are
historical, you can journey back into the city's
past with a visit to the beautiful but forbidding
Peter and Paul Fortress. Leningrad is also the
cradle of the revolution, and you can still see
Lenin's office in the Kseshinskaya Mansion (now
the October Revolution museum) and the
Smolny Institute, from which the Bolsheviks
organised the seizure of power. Leningrad has
always been at the forefront of the nation's
cultural development. Pushkin and Dostoyevsky
walked these streets; so, too, did Tchaikovsky
and Rachmaninov, Pavlova and Nijinsky. Today
you can enjoy the best of the city's opera and

ballet by spending an evening at the Kirov, formerly the Imperial Marinsky Theatre, or by attending a concert at the Philharmonic Hall, named after another distinguished Leningrader, Dimitry Shostakovitch.

It is pretty likely that, at some point in your stay, you will want to go shopping on the famous Nevsky Prospekt, stopping off at Yeliseev's food store, perhaps, or the Gostinny Dvor. In the summer you can stroll through the city's many parks and gardens or take a boat trip on the Neva. Out of town there are the palaces of Pushkin, Petrodvorets and Pavlovsk to wonder at, so you will never be bored.

Weather

Both Moscow and Leningrad are year-round destinations. The winters are cold but invigorating, with frequent snow showers and

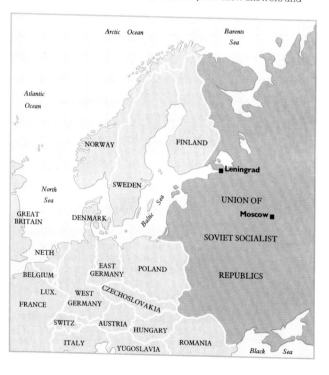

sparkling frosts. Summers have a fair amount of sunshine and the odd sweltering day. Bring a raincoat! If you are lucky enough to visit Leningrad in mid-July you will be able to sample the famous White Nights, when darkness lasts all of 40 minutes and night and day are barely distinguishable.

The Gorbachev Revolution

Since 1985 the Soviet Union has been undergoing a transformation which makes this an especially exciting time to visit. *Perestroika* (restructuring) and *glasnost* (openness) are the current buzzwords. You will not see much sign of improvement in the shops—much to President Gorbachev's dismay—but a number of remarkable changes have taken place. The new Soviet parliament now meets regularly in Moscow, and you may happen to see the MPs trudging across Red Square, stopping occasionally to accept petitions from their constituents; or setting out from the Moskva Hotel, where many of them stay when parliament is in session. Demonstrations are a regular occurrence nowadays, and are no longer automatically broken up by the police. Indeed, protesters have recently placarded the Lubyanka itself, and KGB officials have taken part in a TV phone-in. Propaganda posters pull no punches in denouncing Stalin's crimes, while in 1988 history exams in schools and universities had to be cancelled, owing to the confusion stirred up by current debate. The Orthodox Church recently celebrated the thousandth anniversary of Christianity in Russia by setting up a new headquarters in the Danilovsky Monastery, Moscow, and you can now attend religious services there. Intourist guides are more forthcoming about the country's problems, and are willing to admit that even Lenin made mistakes. The Soviet Union is also encouraging western commerce. You will be able to eat at Pizza Hut and McDonalds. You can shop at Spar, buy your perfume at Estée Lauder or use your credit card in Stockmans inside GUM. In Leningrad you can hire a car from Nissan, drink in bars run by Heineken and OPC-Siemens or buy your jeans at Levi Duty Free. Expect many more changes in the near future.

MOSCOW

BACKGROUND

Set back in Soviet Square, off Gorky Street, one of Moscow's main thoroughfares, is a statue of a warrior on horseback, arm outstretched in command. This is Yury Dolgoruky (George the long-armed), commonly regarded as the founder of Moscow. In 1147, the Russian chronicles tell us, Prince Yury of Suzdal invited a neighbouring prince from Chernigov to a banquet with the words 'Come to me, brother, in Moscow'. In fact, there had already been a settlement here for some time, but not a very important one. Moscow was just one of a number of military outposts in the northern principality of Vladimir-Suzdal, which had been gaining in importance since the decline and fragmentation of the once powerful Kievan state. In Yury's time there were only a few houses and a hunting lodge, and, by 1156, a small wooden fortress or *kreml* (Kremlin), situated near the present Borovitsky Tower at the confluence of the Moskva (Moscow) and Neglinnaya rivers.

Two namesakes merge: Moskva – Moscow city – reflected in the Moskva River

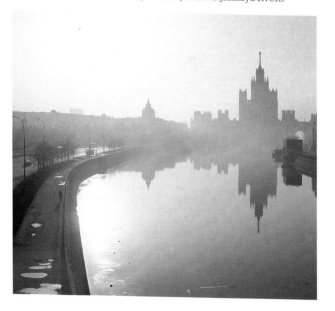

Gold covers the roof of the Kremlin's Cathedral of the Annunciation, a private place of worship and a public display of wealth

The Mongols

Moscow's importance grew out of national catastrophe. In 1237 Batu, grandson of Genghis Khan, unleashed his ferocious Mongol hordes on Russia, crossing the Volga with lightning speed and laying waste everything before him. The following year, Moscow was burnt to the ground and its inhabitants massacred. After Kiev was captured and sacked in 1240, Batu Khan established his capital at Saray on the Volga and all Russia's princes had to appear there to have their titles confirmed. They became tax collectors for their Mongol overlords but were allowed considerable independence within the confines of their territories. The rulers of Moscow exploited this situation to the full, winning the confidence of their conquerors by carrying out their wishes assiduously. In 1276 Prince Daniel, son of the great warrior, Alexander Nevsky, made Moscow his permanent capital and strengthened its defences by building the Danilovsky Monastery,

the first of a series of fortified monasteries
around the periphery of the town, named in this
case after his own patron saint. His successor,
Ivan I, became the first Grand Prince of Moscow
in 1328, a reward for his efficiency as a tax
collector (he was known to his own people as
Kalita, or 'money bag').

Medieval Moscow

Moscow's prestige was further enhanced when
the head of the Orthodox Church, Metropolitan
Peter, transferred the Holy See here from
Vladimir. The town grew quickly in size and
importance. Commanding the trade routes along
the Oka and Volga Rivers, as well as overland
routes from Central Europe, Moscow drew
merchants and commercial travellers like a
magnet. Dealers in fish, furs, hides and cloth all
made their way here, while the labour force was
swelled by fugitives from less politically stable
regions. Noblemen and their retainers,
members of the clergy and soldiers with their
dependants together made up the remainder of
the rapidly growing population. As the grip of
the Mongol occupation began to ease, towards
the end of the 14th century, Moscow grew in
military might and confidence. In 1380, Grand
Prince Dimitry, having received the blessing of
St Sergius, founder of the great monastery of
Sergievo, now Zagorsk, inflicted the first defeat
on the Tatars at the Battle of Kulikovo on the Don
(from which the prince became known as
Dimitry Donskoi). This celebrated victory was
far from marking the end of Mongol
rule—Moscow was burned to the ground in
retaliation only two years later—but it was a step
towards liberation and a powerful hint of what
was to come.

When Ivan III came to the throne in 1462, he
inherited territories eight times greater than a
century before. But he was not one to sit on his
laurels: by the time he died in 1505 Muscovy was
the largest state in Europe, with an area of nearly
500,000 square miles (1,300,000 sq km). Yaroslavl,
Rostov, Tver and Novgorod, all proud and once
independent princedoms, were swallowed up
by their insatiable neighbour. Ivan's writ ran
from the Ural mountains in one direction to the
Arctic Sea in another. At the same time, he

strengthened his dynastic position by marrying Sophia, or Zoë, niece of the last Emperor of Constantinople. The two-headed eagle of Byzantium now became the emblem of the rulers of Russia, and Ivan began to use the title Tsar (Caesar). When Constantinople fell to the Turks in 1453, he went a step further, declaring Moscow to be the third Rome, the new centre of the Orthodox Church. His authority was now absolute, as he revealed to all in 1480 when he ceased paying tribute to the Khan.

Italian Influences

Ivan now turned his attention to the Kremlin and embarked on an ambitious building programme. The cathedrals dating from the time of Dimitry Donskoi were replaced, as foreign architects and craftsmen, mainly from Northern Italy, arrived to supplement the home-grown talent from Pskov, Vladimir and Novgorod. The result was a unique blend of the Renaissance and the East. The Cathedrals of the Annunciation, the Dormition and the Archangel Michael all appeared in the space of little more than twenty years, to be joined by a magnificent new palace, the Palace of the Facets, as it is now called. Meanwhile, the white limestone walls and towers of the Kremlin were pulled down to make way for the present battlements and watchtowers of red brick.

A New Prosperity

Although Moscow remained vulnerable to Tatar attack (the city was captured and burned to the ground in 1571), it continued to grow both in size and prosperity. An English visitor, Giles Fletcher, thought it bigger than London, and there were reckoned to be more than 40,000 houses. The heart of the city, then as now, was the Kremlin, surrounded on three sides by a moat, fed by the Neglinnaya Stream (now running beneath the Alexander Garden in a conduit). Red Square, immediately beyond the Kremlin moat, was a bustling market place; here, too, important announcements were made and executions carried out. There was another trading quarter immediately behind what is now the GUM department store, stretching as far as Dzerzhinsky Square. This area, known as the Kitai-gorod, was surrounded by another stone wall, and there were additional wooden fortifications further out, roughly between the present Boulevard and Garden Rings. There was a large population of labourers and craftsmen, many of whom were employed by the Court. The provisions department alone, for example, employed more than 150 cooks, water carriers, dishwashers and food inspectors while the court stables provided work for an additional 300 servants. Many of the tsar's employees lived in the suburb known as the Arbat, off the modern Kalinin Prospekt, and the street names (Old Stables Lane, Silver Lane, Carpenters Lane) still commemorate the various trades. Another artisan quarter is centred on the present Taganka Square, whose name derives from the kettles used by the tsar's soldiers during their campaigns against the Tatars. There was a settlement of potters here too, while the royal weavers lived further out, at Khamovniki (the Church of St Nicholas in Khamovniki is still known as the Weavers' Church). The skyline of

Russian and Italian architecture are blended in the Cathedral of the Assumption, or the Dormition, a five-domed Kremlin church

16th-century Moscow was, of course, punctuated with gilded onion domes and bell towers, for there were well over 200 churches and 18 religious houses, including the Danilovsky, Don and Andronikov monasteries, which guarded the southern and eastern approaches to the city.

The Time of Troubles

That Moscow continued to flourish during this period is remarkable, given the political turbulence which marked the latter part of the century. The trouble began in the reign of Ivan the Terrible (1533–84). The first ruler of Moscow to be crowned Tsar (in the Uspensky Cathedral), his reign had begun with a number of military successes, the most important of which was the capture of Kazan, which prompted the building of St Basil's Cathedral in Red Square. During the 1560s, however, Ivan turned on the *boyars* (noblemen) who had marred his minority, and his attacks soon degenerated into an irrational and generalised persecution. Gangs of thugs called *oprichniki*, wearing a distinctive black uniform and the badge of a severed dog's head and broom, terrorised the population. Ivan's vicious spells were punctuated with periods of tearful remorse, in which he sent lists of his victims to monasteries so that the monks might remember them in their prayers. His obsession with domestic intrigue was such that he became oblivious to the external threat. His Muscovite subjects suffered the consequences when the Tatars captured and sacked the city in 1571. Worse was to come. The period following Ivan's death in 1584 is known to historians as the Time of Troubles. The feeble Tsar Fyodor was replaced in 1598 by Boris Godunov, who was challenged by a pretender claiming to be Ivan the Terrible's youngest son, Dimitry. A second 'False Dimitry' emerged after Boris' death in 1605 and received military help from the Poles, who occupied Moscow in 1610. Two years later they were ousted by patriotic forces under the leadership of Kuzma Minin, a butcher from Nizhny-Novgorod, and Prince Dimitry Pozharsky. (A statue to both was later erected in Red Square, near St Basil's Cathedral.) The chaos was finally brought to an end in 1613 with the election of Tsar Mikhail Romanov, founder of

The colourful Church of St Nicholas, known as the Weavers' Church after the royal weavers who once lived in the area

the dynasty which was to survive until the revolution.

The 17th century saw the continued expansion of the Russian Empire. Part of the Ukraine as far as the River Dnieper (and including the city of Kiev) was acquired in 1667 and the colonisation of Siberia went on apace. By 1700 Russian settlers had reached Okhotsk on the Pacific coast, and clashed for the first time with the Chinese on the Amur River.

The Russians did not have it all their own way. In 1669 the Don cossacks, led by Stenka Razin, launched a rebellion which took government forces almost two years to quell. In June 1671, however, Razin was finally captured, brought to Moscow and drawn and quartered in Red Square: Ulitsa Razina, between St Basil's and the Rossia Hotel, marks the route of his last journey

Moscow Neglected

During the reign of Peter the Great (1682–1725) Russia's attention shifted northwards toward the Baltic, with damaging consequences for Moscow. The new city of St Petersburg (now Leningrad) was officially declared the capital in 1712, two years before another decree forbade building in stone in any other city. Ironically, Peter's obsession with Westernisation can be traced back to his youth in Moscow, when he was irresistibly drawn to the Foreigner's Quarter (Nemetskaya Sloboda), near the modern Kursk Railway Station. The two regiments of which he was most proud, the Preobrazhensky and Semyonovsky Guards, were also named after Moscow villages.

Moscow was not wholly eclipsed by the new northern capital. During Peter's reign the nobility were compelled to live in St Petersburg, but after his death there was a wholesale exodus south from its bleak and inhospitable shores. A period of concentrated building followed. Fine new mansions and town houses, built originally in wood and later in stone, began to transform the Arbat and Prechistenka ('the cleanest') districts into 'nests of the gentry'. The fabulously wealthy Sheremetiev family used serf labour to

Moscow State University, built in the imposing Gothic style favoured by Stalin

develop their out-of-town estates at Ostankino (near the Park of Economic Achievements) and Kuskovo, while the Golitsyns and Yussupovs followed suit at Arkhangelskoye. New thoroughfares, like the Tverskaya (now Gorky Street), were opened up, two large hospitals were constructed and Russia's first university founded just across from the Alexander Garden in 1775. One project, fortunately, was not realised. This was Catherine the Great's plan for a huge new classical palace to replace the Kremlin. In the end only the architect's model was completed, though a number of important buildings were demolished to clear the site.

War and Peace

Napoleon's grim sojourn in Moscow is brilliantly described in Tolstoy's *War and Peace*. The hut where Kutuzov and the other Russian generals deliberated on the eve of his entry has been preserved in a building on Kutuzovsky Prospekt. When the French were compelled to evacuate the city, Napoleon gave orders for the Kremlin, the Novodevichy Convent and other important buildings to be blown up, but Russian troops arrived just in time to prevent this disaster. They were unable, however, to do anything about the great fire which started mysteriously and is said to have consumed more than 80 per cent of Moscow's predominantly wooden houses. Reconstruction, mainly in brick, began immediately, and some of the city's finest buildings and squares date from this period. The Manege, formerly a military riding school and now an exhibition centre, was completed to a French design in 1825. Theatre (now Sverdlov) Square, with its magnificent centrepiece, the Bolshoi Theatre, dates from the same period, as does the Alexander Garden, laid out over the fetid Neglinnaya stream in 1821. New thoroughfares like Prechistenka, now Kropotkin Street, were planned so that the Orlovs, the Lopukhins and the Naryshkins could adorn them with Empire-style mansions.

Moscow Transformed

Much more dramatic changes occurred during the second half of the century as Moscow responded to the government's twin goals of

The palatial underground railway in Moscow gives a grandiose touch to commuting

modernisation and industrialisation. The city was a vibrant financial and commercial centre and, with its nine railway stations, the hub of Russia's communications network. The population of 350,000 in 1840 increased to just over a million in 1900, making Moscow the 10th largest city in the world. By this time, two-thirds of the inhabitants (mostly peasants from the surrounding countryside) lived outside the city proper in poorly lit and ill-paved factory 'suburbs'—little shanty towns separated by acres of neglected waste ground. But factories and workshops invaded the central districts, too, their belching chimneys casting a grimy pall over once resplendent buildings. There were a number of 'no go' areas, like the Khitrov market near the Rossia Hotel and a notorious red light district, northeast of the Bolshoi Theatre. Yet there were still country lanes twisting through the Arbat, complete with grassy courtyards, kitchen gardens, stables, even cocks and hens. Not for nothing was Moscow known as the 'big village'. There were plenty of pleasant green spaces outside the city, too—Sokolniki Park, for example, or Sparrow (now Lenin) Hills.

Revolution and Civil War

Fierce fighting took place in Moscow during the
Revolution of 1905, when workers and
revolutionaries set up barricades in the Presnya
district, near the Barrikadnaya Metro station. In
November 1917 the Bolshevik seizure of power
was more violent here than in Petersburg, with
shooting in Red Square and around the Arbat,
and running battles between workers and
troops. Lenin moved the capital back to Moscow
in March 1918 and stayed for a few days in the
National Hotel, before taking up residence in the
Kremlin. During the ensuing Civil War, the city
was plunged into anarchy and Lenin himself was
held up by armed bandits while on a drive
through the suburbs, early in 1919.

Stalin's Imprint

Stalin's Plan for the Reconstruction of Moscow
envisaged cutting a swathe through several of
the old districts and demolishing countless
buildings of historical interest. Marx Prospekt,
the widened Gorky Street, Leninsky Prospekt
and Prospekt Mira all date from this period, as
does the lavish Metro system. In October 1941
the government evacuated Moscow in the face
of the Nazi advance, but the invading forces
were driven back from the outskirts of the city in
what was one of the major turning points of the
war.

Moscow Today

The postwar period has been one of continued,
planned expansion, with suburbs relentlessly
pushing out the frontiers of the city. The result is
a rather soulless panorama of identical tower
blocks stretching far into the distance. There
have been comparatively few changes in the
city centre. Stalin's famous 'wedding cake'
buildings (the University at Lenin Hills and the
Ministry of Foreign Affairs, for example) date
from the 1940s and 1950s, while the new Kalinin
Prospekt is a '60s development. More
heartening than these Brave New World efforts
has been the recent emphasis on restoration and
preservation, the best example being the soon
to be reopened Metropole Hotel. The sight of
Western shop fronts, such as Estée Lauder in
Gorky Street, is another novelty.

WHAT TO SEE

Western visitors often come away disappointed from Soviet museums, not because the exhibits are uninteresting—they are often fascinating—but because of the unimaginative presentation. That said, there are some first-rate museums in Moscow (the Novodevichy Convent for example) and the art galleries are among the finest in the world. Below is a list of the most important ones, together with a selection from the more specialised collections. If your own special interest is not catered for here, ask Intourist for more information. Opening times are the latest available but check before you set out, as there are seasonal and other variations. Unless you are visiting with a tour group, take a detailed guidebook with you—many

The Pushkin Museum of Fine Art (see page 29) houses a celebrated collection of French paintings

museums, especially the smaller ones, mark exhibits in Russian only.

Museums and Art Galleries

ALEXANDER PUSHKIN MUSEUM
Ulitsa Kropotkinskaya 12/2
Dedicated to the life and work of Russia's greatest poet, who died following a duel in 1837. Period house and furnishings, together with paintings, letters and first editions of Pushkin's works. Pleasing, but not as evocative as its Leningrad equivalent.
Open: Saturday 13.00 to 19.30 hrs; Sunday 11.00 to 17.30 hrs
Closed: Monday to Friday
Metro: Kropotkinskaya

ANDRONIKOV MONASTERY; ANDREI RUBLYOV MUSEUM OF OLD RUSSIAN ART

Ploshchad Pryamikova 10
One of several monastery fortresses guarding the approaches to Moscow, the Andronikov was founded by the Metropolitan Alexey in 1359. The beautifully proportioned white stone building is the Cathedral of the Saviour, dating from 1427. Other buildings worthy of note are the refectory (early 16th century) and the Church of the Archangel Michael and St Alexius (1694–1739), a fine example of Naryshkin Baroque. Andrei Rublyov, one of the greatest Russian icon painters, was a monk here. Most of his finest work is now in the Tretyakov Gallery and only traces can be seen in the Cathedral. However, the museum does contain some splendid icons dating from the 15th to 18th centuries, including a work by Dionysius.
Open: daily 10.00 to 18.00 hrs
Closed: Wednesdays and last Friday of each month
Metro: Ploshchad Ilyicha

BAKHRUSHIN THEATRE MUSEUM

Ulitsa Bakhrushina 31/12
More than 200,000 photos, posters, programmes and personal effects illustrating the history of the Russian stage from the 18th century to the present. Items of special interest include Chaliapin's costume for *Boris Godunov* and Nijinsky's dancing shoes. A fascinating collection, unimaginatively displayed.

Open: Monday, Thursday, Saturday, Sunday 12.00 to 19.00 hrs; Wednesday and Friday 14.00 to 21.00 hrs
Closed: Tuesdays and last Monday of each month
Metro: Paveletskaya

BORODINO PANORAMA MUSEUM

Kutuzovsky Prospekt 38
Commemorates the famous battle of August 1812, which was actually fought about 78 miles (125km) to the west of Moscow. The confrontation between the Russian and French forces, which ended in stalemate, is depicted in a 370-foot (115m)-long painting by Franz Roubaud, commissioned to mark its centenary. Close by the museum you can see an exact replica of the hut where Marshal Kutuzov finally decided to abandon Moscow to the French.
Open: daily except Fridays 09.30 to 20.00 hrs (summer) and 10.30 to 19.00 hrs (winter)
Closed: last Thursday of each month
Metro: Kutuzovskaya

CENTRAL LENIN MUSEUM

Ploshchad Revolyutsii 2
All you will ever need to know about the great revolutionary leader and founder of the modern Soviet state. The 13,000 exhibits include manuscripts and first editions, letters, photos, paintings and other memorabilia. Also on display are Lenin's official car (a 1914 Rolls-Royce Silver Ghost) and a replica of his office in the Kremlin.
Open: Tuesday to Thursday 11.00 to 19.30 hrs; Friday to

Sunday 10.00 to 18.30 hrs
Closed: Mondays and last
Tuesday of each month
Metro: Ploshchad
Revolyutsii/Ploshchad
Sverdlova/Prospekt Marksa

CENTRAL MUSEUM OF THE REVOLUTION

Ulitsa Gorkogo 21
The stone lions guarding the
entrance to this museum
—formerly the English Club, a
favourite haunt of the
aristocracy—are mentioned by
Pushkin in his poem *Eugene
Onyegin.* The exhibition now
consists of a somewhat
overwhelming array of
documents, photos, paintings
and objects relating to the
revolution of 1905 and the
February and October
revolutions of 1917. A full-
blooded celebration of Soviet
socialism, not for the faint-
hearted!
Open: Tuesdays and
Wednesdays 12.00 to 20.00 hrs;
Thursdays and Sundays 10.00 to
18.00 hrs; Fridays 11.00 to
19.00 hrs
Closed: Mondays
Metro: Mayakovskaya

◆◆
CHEKHOV HOUSE MUSEUM

Sadovaya-Kudrinskaya Ulitsa, 6
Chekhov lived here from
1886–90, when he decided to
give up practising medicine to
become a full-time writer. The
study, which contains a number
of his personal possessions, is
where he wrote his first play,
Ivanov, and many of his short
stories.
Open: Tuesdays, Thursdays,
Saturdays and Sundays 11.00 to

18.00 hrs; Wednesdays and
Fridays14.00 to 21.00 hrs
Closed: Mondays
Metro: Barrikadnaya

◆
DON MONASTERY: SHCHUSEV MUSEUM OF ARCHITECTURE

Donskaya Ploshchad 1
Founded by Boris Godunov in
1591 on the site of the last major
confrontation between the Tatars
and Muscovites. The Old
Cathedral has a copy of the Don
Virgin icon, from which the
monastery takes its name. The
New Cathedral and the
defensive walls which surround
it were built by Peter the Great's
sister, Sofiya, in the late 17th
century. The church contains an
impressive iconostasis (screen)
and frescos by Antonio Claudio.
The circular gallery houses part
of the Shchusev Museum of
Architecture, comprising
sketches, plans, photographs
and other materials illustrating
the history of Russian
architecture from the time of
Peter the Great. Also within the
grounds are the Church of the
Archangel Michael, where
members of the powerful
Golitsyn family lie buried, and
the Gate Church of the Virgin of
Tikhvin.
Open: Tuesday to Friday,
Sunday 11.00 to 18.00 hrs
Closed: Mondays, Saturdays and
the last Thursday of the month
Metro: Shabolovskaya

EXHIBITION OF ECONOMIC ACHIEVEMENTS OF THE USSR (VDNKh)

Prospekt Mira
Upbeat and distinctly pre-
glasnost celebration of the

achievements of Soviet socialism, which your Intourist guide will be only too eager to show you. The exhibition occupies a 750-acre (300-hectare) site and there are 80 pavilions covering agriculture, industry, science, technology, and much more besides. If you are interested in space exploration, head straight for the Space Museum, near the Metro and in the shadow of the 300-foot (90m)-high Sputnik Obelisk. Inside the exhibition there are cafés, cinemas, an open-air theatre and a fun fair for the children.
Open: daily 10.00 to 21.00 hrs
Metro: VDNKh

An economic achievement on display: Russian space and aviation technology in the Space Museum

◆
GLINKA MUSEUM OF MUSICAL CULTURE
Ulitsa Fadeyeva 4
Named after the founder of modern Russian music, Milkhail Glinka, the museum houses musical instruments, together with scores, letters and other items relating to the great Russian and Western composers of the 18th and 19th centuries.
Open: Mondays and Thursdays 14.00 to 22.00 hrs; Wednesdays, Friday to Sunday 11.00 to 19.00 hrs
Closed: Tuesdays and last Friday of each month
Metro: Mayakovskaya

◆◆
KUSKOVO ESTATE MUSEUM
Ulitsa Yunosti 2
The Sheremetiev family, who

CENTRAL MOSKVA

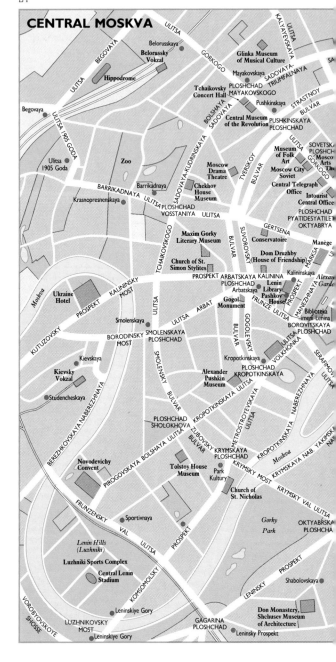

ULITSA

ULITSA KALYAYEVSKAYA

SA

Belorusskaya

Belorussky Vokzal

GORKOGO

Glinka Museum of Musical Culture

Mayakovskaya

SADOVAYA-TRIUMFALNAYA

BEGOVAYA

Hippodrome

ULITSA

Tchaikovsky Concert Hall

PLOSHCHAD MAYAKOVSKOGO

BOLSHAYA SADOVAYA

STRASTNOY BULVAR

Pushkinskaya

PUSHKINSKAYA PLOSHCHAD

Begovaya

ULITSA 1905 GODA

Central Museum of the Revolution

SOVETSKA PLOSHCH

Museum of Folk Art

Mosco

GORKOGO

Zoo

Ulitsa 1905 Goda

SADOVAYA-KUDRINSKAYA

Moscow Drama Theatre

TVERSKOY

BULVAR

Moscow City Soviet

Th

Central Telegraph Office

BARRIKADNAYA ULITSA

Barrikadnaya

Chekhov House Museum

Intourist Central Office

Krasnopresnenskaya

PLOSHCHAD VOSSTANIYA ULITSA

PLOSHCHAD PYATIDESYATILE OKTYABRYA

GERTSENA

SUVOROVSK

Maxim Gorky Literary Museum

BULVAR

Conservatoire

Manège

TCHAIKOVSKOGO

Church of St. Simon Stylites

Dom Druzhby (House of Friendship)

MARSA

U

PROSPEKT ARBATSKAYA KALININA PLOSHCHAD

Kalininskaya

Alexan Garde

Ukraine Hotel

KALININSKY MOST

ULITSA

Arbatskaya

Lenin Library

PROSPEKT

MANEZHNAYA

KUTUZOVSKY

PROSPEKT

ULITSA ARBAT

Gogol Monument

Pashkov House

FRUNZE ULITSA

Biblioteka imeni Lenina

Smolenskaya

GOGOLEVSKY

BOROVITSKAYA PLOSHCHAD

Moskva

BORODINSKY MOST

SMOLENSKAYA PLOSHCHAD

BULVAR

ULITSA VOLKHONKA

SERAFIMOV

Kievskaya

SMOLENSKY

Kropotkinskaya

NABEREZHNAYA

ULITSA

Kievsky Vokzal

BULVAR

PLOSHCHAD KROPOTKINSKAYA

Studencheskaya

Alexander Pushkin Museum

KROPOTKINSKAYA ULITSA

METROSTROYEVSKAYA ULITSA

KROPOTKINSKAYA

Moskva

KROPOTKINSKAYA NAB. YAKYMSK

NA

BEREZHKOVSKAYA NABEREZHNAYA

PLOSHCHAD SHOLOKHOVA

ZUBOVSKY BULVAR

BOLSHAYA ULITSA

KRYMSKAYA PLOSHCHAD

KRYMSKY MOST

KRYMSKAYA NAB.

Novodevichy Convent

PIROGOVSKAYA

Tolstoy House Museum

Park Kultury

KRYMSKY VAL ULITSA

Church of St. Nicholas

FRUNZENSKY

VAL

Sportivnaya

PROSPEKT

Gorky Park

OKTYABRSKA PLOSHCHAD

ULITSA

Lenin Hills (Luzhniki)

Luzhniki Sports Complex

Central Lenin Stadium

KOMSOMOLSKY

PROSPEKT

LENINSKY

Shabolovskaya

VOROBYOVSKOYE

SHOSSE

LUZHNIKOVSKY MOST

Leninskiye Gory

GAGARINA PLOSHCHAD

Leninsky Prospekt

Don Monastery, Shchusev Museum of Architecture

Leninskiye Gory

Central Puppet Theatre

Prospekt Mira

PROSPEKT MIRA

Yaroslavsky Vokzal

GAZOYSKAYA

BAKUNINSKAYA ULITSA

VAYA-HNAYA

SADOVAYA-SUKHAREVSKAYA

Kolkhoznaya

Leningradsky Vokzal

Krasnoselskaya

KOMSOMOLSKAYA PLOSHCHAD

ULITSA

OVSKY

ROZHDESTVENSKA

SADOVAYA-SPASSKAYA

PROSPEKT

Komsomolskaya

VAR

TRUBNAYA PLOSHCHAD

BULVAR

ULITSA

STRETENKA

NOVO KIROVSY

ULITSA

Lermontovskaya

LERMONTOVSKAYA PLOSHCHAD

Baumanskaya

Maly Theatre

NEGLINNAYA

STRETENSKY

Turgenevskaya

KIROVA

SADOVAYA

KARL MARX ULITSA

TROVKA

Kuznetsky Most

Church of St. Louis

BULVAR TURGENEVESKAYA PLOSHCHAD

CHERNOGRYAZSKAYA

oire

Detsky Mir (Children's World)

DZERZHINSKOGO

ULITSA KIROVA

Kirovskaya

CHRISTOPRUDNY

oshchad Sverdlova

PLOSHCHAD MARKSA

ULITSA

Mayakovsky House Museum

PROSPEKT

DZERZHINSKOGO

Ploshchad Revolyutsii

Dzerzhinskaya

NOVAYA PLOSHCHAD

PROYEZD

BULVAR

CHERNYSHEVSKOGO

CHKALOVA

Kurskaya

otel oskva

PLOSHCHAD REVOLYUTSII

Central Lenin Museum

GUM Department Store

Ploshchad Nogina

POKROVSKY

Kursky Vokzal

Historical Museum

Lenin Mausoleum

ULITSA KUIBYSHEVA

SEROVA STAMAYA PLOSHCHAD

ULITSA

Ploshchad Nogina

BULVAR

YAUSKY

mlin

KRASNAYA PLOSHCHAD (RED SQUARE)

ULITSA RAZINA

PLOSHCHAD NOGINA

SOYANKA

CHKALOVA

St. Basil's Cathedral

Rossia Hotel

MOSKVORETSKY

ULITSA

Andronikov Monastery, Andrei Rublyov Museum

LYOVSKAYA NABEREZHNAYA

MOST

MOSKVORETSKAYA NAB.

ASTACHOV MOST

ULYANOVSKAYA

ULITSA

Taganka Theatre

INTERNALYNAYA ULITSA

ULITSA

TAGANSKAYA PLOSHCHAD

Tretyakov Gallery

ULITSA

ORDYNKA

Novokuznetskaya

Taganskaya

TAGANSKAYA ULITSA

NARODNAYA

ULITSA MARKSISTSKAYA

Marksistskaya

AYA POLYANKA ULITSA

BOLSHAYA

Bakhrushin Theatre Museum

KRASNOKHOLMSKY MOST

Proletarskaya

SINOMOVSKY PROSPEKT

VOLGOGRADSKY PROSPEKT

DOBRYNINSKAYA

abrskaya PLOSHCHAD

LENINSKAYA PLOSHCHAD

VALOVAYA ULITSA

Paveletskaya

NOVOSPASSKY MOST

SARINSKY

VAL

ULITSA

RYNINSKAYA ULITSA

Dobryninskaya

ULITSA

Paveletsky Vokzal

AYA

ULITSA

LYUSINOVSKAYA

DUBININSKAYA

Moskva

Danilovskaya

Danilov Monastery

0   1 kilometre

0   1 mile

built this estate, once owned 200,000 serfs and more than three million acres (1,200,000 hectares) of land. The two-storey wooden palace dates from 1777 and the interior is decorated with a dazzling array of paintings, tapestries and mirrors. It now functions as a Ceramics Museum. Other buildings of note include the Dutch and Italian houses, the Hermitage (in French style) and the Grotto. Sheremetiev's celebrated company of serf actors performed in the open-air theatre near the orangery.

Open: Tuesday to Friday 11.00 to 19.00 hrs; Saturday, Sunday 10.00 to 18.00 hrs
Closed: Mondays
Metro: Zhdanovskaya

◆
MAXIM GORKY LITERARY MUSEUM
Ulitsa Vorovskogo 25a
Devoted to the life and work of Russia's best known socialist writer, the museum, an Empire Style building of the 1820s, formerly belonged to the Director of the Imperial Theatres. On display is an

*The gleaming white and gold of
Novodevichy Convent, a religious
house and occasional prison*

impressive collection of
manuscripts, letters,
photographs and first editions
relating to the author of *The
Lower Depths*, *Mother* and *My
Childhood*. The more imposing
mansion at no 50 is reputed to be
the home of the Rostovs in
Tolstoy's novel *War and Peace*.
Open: Tuesdays and Fridays
08.00 to 20.00 hrs; Wednesdays,
Thursdays and Sundays 10.00 to
17.00 hrs

Closed: Mondays
Metro: Arbatskaya

◆
MAYAKOVSKY HOUSE-
MUSEUM
Proyezd Serova 3/6
This is where Vladimir
Mayakovsky, Futurist poet,
playwright and revolutionary,
lived from 1919, and where he
shot himself 11 years later at the
age of 37. The museum contains
manuscripts, posters, first
editions and personal effects,
and there are occasional film
shows.
Open: Mondays and Thursdays
12.00 to 20.00 hrs; Tuesdays,
Friday to Sunday 10.00 to
18.00 hrs
Closed: Wednesdays
Metro: Dzerzhinskaya

◆
MUSEUM OF FOLK ART
Ulitsa Stanislavskogo 7
On display here are some of the
finest examples of Russian arts
and crafts, including *palekh*
(lacquer painting), ceramics,
wood and metal work,
glassware, prints, lace and
embroidery, all dating from the
17th century onwards.
Open: Tuesdays and Thursdays
14.00 to 20.00 hrs; Wednesday,
Friday to Sunday 11.00 to
17.00 hrs
Closed: Mondays and the last
day of each month
Metro: Pushkinskaya, Ploshchad
Revolyutsii

◆◆◆
NOVODEVICHY CONVENT
Novodevichy Proyezd 1
You will be dazzled by this
architectural gem, with its

crenellated walls of white brick, red-capped towers and gleaming onion domes. Founded by Basil III in 1524 to commemorate the capture of Smolensk from the Lithuanians, the convent developed into one of Russia's major religious houses, served almost exclusively by daughters of the nobility. Boris Godunov was proclaimed tsar here in 1598 and, a century later, Peter the Great had his half-sister, Sofia, imprisoned within its walls for conspiring against him. When

Created by serfs in the 18th century, the Ostankino Palace Museum of Serf Art is a show of craftsmanship and splendour; the rich Sheremetievs owned the estate

Napoleon arrived in 1812 he gave orders for the convent to be blown up but, at the last moment, the nuns managed to extinguish the fuses.

The Smolensk Cathedral is the oldest part of the convent and contains some exquisite late 16th-century frescos, a magnificent five-tier iconostasis dating from 1683–6 and a copper font of the same period. Bibles, vestments, silver and other religious treasures are also on view here.

The church of the Dormition, which is open for worship, and the refectory were built in 1685–7. The two Gate Churches, which dominate the northern and southern entrances of the convent, and the 17th-century bell-tower are also worth a look. Just outside the walls is the cemetery, final resting place of Gogol, Chekhov, Eisenstein, Prokofiev, Stanislavsky and the former Soviet leader, Nikita Khrushchev.

Open: 1 May to 31 October Mondays, Wednesday to Sunday 10.00 to 18.00 hrs; 1 November to 30 April 10.00 to 17.00 hrs
Closed: Tuesdays and last day of each month
Metro: Sportivnaya

OSTANKINO PALACE MUSEUM OF SERF ART
Pervaya Ostankinskaya Ulitsa, 5
This estate, like Kuskovo (see page 23) belonged to the fabulously wealthy Sheremetiev family. The wooden palace was designed and constructed entirely by serf labour between 1792 and 1798. The interior is a magnificent tribute to these artists and craftsmen. You will marvel at the parquetry, the decorative carvings and the finely wrought crystal chandeliers, and these provide a splendid backdrop to the collection of 18th-century furniture, paintings, porcelain and crystal. Sheremetiev's company of 200 actors, all serfs, performed in the purpose-built theatre which, thanks to a device which raised the auditorium, also served as a ballroom. You can also enjoy a stroll in the palace grounds and a visit to the Church of the Trinity, commissioned by a previous owner of the estate in 1687. Adjacent to the park are the Botanical Gardens of the Academy of Sciences.
Open: 1 October–3 May: Mondays, Thursday to Sunday 10.00 to 14.00 hrs;
May–September: 11.00 to 17.00 hrs
Closed: Tuesdays and Wednesdays
Metro: VDNKh

PUSHKIN MUSEUM OF FINE ART
Ulitsa Volkhonka 12
This museum is renowned for its collection of French painting, especially of the Impressionist and Post-Impressionist schools. It was founded in 1912, but most of the great works of art now on display were acquired after the Revolution, when the Soviet Government nationalised the private collections of the textile magnates, S I Shchukin, Savva Morozov and other wealthy connoisseurs. If time is short, head for Rooms 17, 18 and 21 on

the First Floor, where you will find masterpieces like Manet's *Dejeuner sur l'Herbe* and some of Monet's Rouen Cathedral pictures, as well as paintings by Renoir, Degas, Cézanne, Gauguin, Matisse and some early Picassos. Room 23 (also on the First Floor) displays French and English painting from the early 19th century, including works by Corot, Delacroix and Constable. If you still have time to spare, return to the Ground Floor, where you can choose from among Botticelli and Veronese (Room 5) Rubens, Rembrandt and Van Dyck (Rooms 8–10) Murillo and Goya (Room 11) and the French Schools of the 17th and 18th centuries (Room 13). The Pushkin also displays an impressive array of antiquities from Egypt, the Near East, Rome and Byzantium.
Open: Tuesday to Sunday 10.00 to 20.00 hrs
Closed: Mondays
Metro: Kropotkinskaya

SOVIET ARMED FORCES MUSEUM
Ulitsa Sovietskoi Armii 2
Everything for the military buff. The museum traces the history and development of the Soviet Armed Forces from the Revolution onwards, with special emphasis on the Great Patriotic War (World War II). Among the exhibits are sections of the American U-2 reconnaissance plane brought down over Siberia in 1960, causing President Eisenhower much embarrassment.
Open: Tuesday, Friday to

Sunday 10.00 to 17.00 hrs; Wednesdays and Thursdays 13.00 to 20.00 hrs
Closed: Mondays and last Tuesday of each month
Metro: Prospekt Mira

TOLSTOY HOUSE MUSEUM
Ulitsa Lva Tolstova 21
Tolstoy bought this house in 1882 and wintered here each year until 1901 (his summers were spent at Yasnaya Polyana, an estate about 120 miles (200km) south of Moscow). Sixteen rooms have been preserved as the author left them, including the study where he wrote *Resurrection*, *The Death of Ivan Ilyich* and *The Kreutzer Sonata*.
Open: Tuesday to Sunday 10.00 to 17.00 hrs (you must be shown round by a guide—see Intourist for details)
Closed: Mondays and last day of each month
Metro: Park Kultury

TRETYAKOV GALLERY
Lavrushinsky Pereulok 10
The greatest single collection of Russian art in the world, presented to the city of Moscow by the merchant P M Tretyakov, in 1892. The Gallery itself dates from 1900–5 and was designed by Victor Vasnetsov in a style best described as Russian Art Nouveau.
The Tretyakov has almost 50,000 paintings on exhibition, so you will have to be selective! As it is most famous for its unrivalled collection of icons, dating back to the 11th century, you are probably best advised to start with Rooms 38 and 39 on the Ground Floor. Here you will find

Named after Tsar Alexander I, Alexander Garden was laid out over the Neglinnaya River in the early 19th century

masterpieces by each of the great trio of Russian icon painters: Andrei Rublyov, Dionysius and Theophanes the Greek.

Your next port of call should be the First Floor, starting with Room 11, which deals with the work of the Peredvizhniki or Itinerants, a group of rebel artists of the 1870s, whose founder members included Ivan Kramskoy, Vasily Perov (don't miss his famous portrait of Dostoyevsky) and Fyodor Vasilyev. The itinerants turned their back on Western fashions

in order to concentrate instead
on Russian themes. The greatest
of them were Ilya Repin, whose
best known paintings, including
*Religious Procession in Kursk
Province, Unexpected Return of
a Political Exile* and *Ivan the
Terrible and His Son*, can be
found in Rooms 25 and 26; and

*This intriguing scene is actually the
window display of a pet supplies
shop in Arbat, an area once home to
the tsar's servants*

Isaac Levitan, famous for his
landscapes, which you will find
in Room 29, back on the Ground
Floor. Rooms 30–33 (also on the

Ground Floor) are devoted to paintings by two other artists not to be missed—Mikhail Vrubel and Valentin Serov.
Still not exhausted? Then you might like to finish off with some modern art. The Tretyakov collection includes canvases by internationally known artists like Marc Chagall, Kazimir Malevich and Vasily Kandinsky, as well as lesser known painters, such as Kuzma Petrov-Vodkin. At the time of writing the Tretyakov Gallery is closed for restoration. It is due to reopen in 1991.
Metro: Novokuznetskaya

Other Places of Interest

◆
ALEXANDER GARDEN
Manezhnaya Ulitsa
Easily combined with a visit to Red Square. Walk through the gap between the Historical Museum and the Kremlin Wall (opposite St Basil's), turn left and you're there. Beneath you is the Neglinnaya River, which once formed part of the Kremlin moat (a stone bridge still links the Kutafya and Trinity towers, which you can see ahead). The river was covered over in 1817 and the Gardens, named after Tsar Alexander I, were laid out shortly afterwards. By the gate is the Tomb of the Unknown Soldier, guarded by an eternal flame. It is a custom for newly married couples to lay flowers here immediately after their wedding. A little further on is the Obelisk to Revolutionary Thinkers, originally a monument to the Romanov Dynasty, which celebrated its tercentenary in 1913, but re-designed immediately after the Revolution

(the double-headed Imperial eagle was first to go). Continue your stroll through the Gardens and you will eventually come to the Borovitskaya Tower, one of the public entrances to the Kremlin. Across the road is the **Pashkov House and Lenin Library** and you are also within easy walking distance of the **Manège**.

ARBAT
The easiest way to reach this delightful part of old Moscow is to walk up Prospekt Kalinina and turn left just after the overpass, near the Prague Restaurant. Alternatively, take the Metro and alight at Arbatskaya. This is an area for strolling in, either in the daytime or of an evening. Arbat Street itself, now pedestrianised, was once Moscow's leading shopping street; now it's a favourite haunt of pavement artists, street poets and musicians. There are bookshops for browsing in and you can buy your Russian posters from **Iskusstvo** (Ul. Arbat 4) at 10 kopeks a time. The neighbouring streets all have picturesque names: Silver Lane, Biscuit Lane, Carpenters' Lane, Old Stables Lane: a throwback to the days when the Tsar's servants lived here. Later the area was taken over by the aristocracy and some of their imposing residences can still be seen. The Arbat has strong literary associations: Pushkin lived at no 53 for a while, and Gogol's house, 7 Suvorovsky Bulvar, is also close by. (There is a famous monument to Gogol near the Metro station.)

BOLSHOI THEATRE/SVERDLOV SQUARE
Ploshchad Sverdlova

There has been a theatre on this site since 1780, although the present neo-classical building dates only from the middle of the 19th century. The rather striking bronze quadriga above the portico represents Apollo's chariot being pulled by four horses. The Bolshoi is, of course, the home of the internationally famous opera and ballet company of the same name. The square, formerly Theatre Square, was renamed after the revolution in honour of the first Soviet President, Iakov Sverdlov. A statue of Karl Marx stands in the centre. To the right of the theatre is the Maly or small theatre (so called to distinguish it from the Bolshoi, which means big) and to the left, opposite the Maly, is the Children's Theatre.

DZERZHINSKY SQUARE
Ploshchad Dzerzhinskogo

A short walk from the Kremlin along Marx Prospekt, or take the Metro (Dzerzhinskaya). The square is named after the founder of the Soviet secret police, Felix Dzerzhinsky (actually a Pole). His statue stands in the centre. To the left is **Detskii Mir**, the children's department store. Opposite, by Kirov Street, is the infamous Lubyanka, headquarters of the KGB and once the offices of an insurance company. Tucked away on Malaya Lubyanka Street is the charming Roman Catholic Church of **St Louis**, built in 1830.

GORKY STREET
Ulitsa Gorkogo

The street begins near Prospekt Marksa Metro Station. Once known as Tver Street, a narrow twisting lane heading into the countryside, it was widened in the 1930s and renamed after the Socialist writer, Maxim Gorky. The skyscraper to your left is the Intourist Hotel. On the next street corner you will see a large, grey building with a revolving globe: this is the Central Telegraph Office. Opposite, on the street called Proyezd Khudozhestvennovo Teatra, is the **Moscow Arts Theatre**, where Chekhov's play *The Cherry Orchard* was first performed. A short walk will bring you to Soviet Square. On the right is the equestrian statue of Prince Yuri Dolgoruky, the founder of Moscow, and opposite is the building of the Moscow City Soviet, in Tsarist times the residence of the Governor-General. Continue along Gorky Street, past the Central Hotel, and you will come to the famous food store, once known as Yeliseev's and now, more functionally, as **Gastronom No 1**. Pop in to admire the luxurious late 19th-century décor. A little further on is **Pushkin Square**. A statue honouring the famous poet stands in the centre. You will also see the gigantic Rossia Cinema and the offices of *Izvestiya* and the Novosti press agency. Pass the Metro station and on your left are the railings and gateway of what was formerly the English Club, an exclusive haunt of the nobility. Pushkin mentions the stone lions in his poem *Eugene Onyegin*. This elegant classical building is now The Central Museum of the Revolution. You could end your walk at **Mayakovsky Square**, named in honour of the Soviet

The neo-classical Bolshoi Theatre lives up to its name – which means Big Theatre

poet, Vladimir Mayakovsky. The **Tchaikovsky Concert Hall** is on the corner, next to the Metro station.

◆◆
KALININ PROSPEKT
Prospekt Kalinina
This brave new world of a street starts at Prospekt Marksa. The

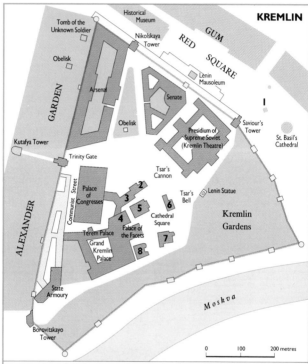

KREMLIN

1 Monument to Minin and Pozharsky
2 Cathedral of the Twelve Apostles
3 Patriach's Palace
4 Church of the Deposition of the Robe
5 Cathedral of the Assumption
6 Ivan the Great Bell Tower
7 Cathedral of the Archangel Michael
8 Cathedral of the Annunciation

ornate building at no 14 is **Dom Druzhby** (House of Friendship). Formerly the home of the Moscow millionaire industrialist, Savva Morozov, it is deliberately eclectic in style, combining classical with Renaissance and baroque features. Cross the huge underpass at Suvorov Boulevard and you will see the Prague Restaurant on your left, the starting point of the **Arbat** district. On your right, just past

Communications House, is the charming 17th-century church of **St Simon Stylites**, now, alas, looking sadly out of place. The huge tower blocks which now overshadow it house a number of useful shops. In the first block are the Malachite jewellery shop and Dom Knigi (house of books). Further on you will find the Melodiya record store. Across the street are more shops and offices, including the Zhiguli beer hall and, much further on, on the corner of Tchaikovsky Street, the Arbat restaurant. If you continue to walk as far as the Kalinin Bridge, you will come to the Ukraine Hotel and Kutuzovsky Prospekt.

◆◆◆
KREMLIN
Kreml
You can visit the Kremlin on your own, or you can join a guided tour organised by Intourist. The first alternative is cheaper. (You can buy tickets from the *kassa*, ticket office, in the main courtyard.) However, you may have to join a lengthy queue to see the State Armoury and, as this is one of the main attractions, equivalent to viewing the Crown Jewels in the Tower of London, you may decide it is worth paying Intourist to guarantee you immediate access to all buildings open to the public.
The main entrance to the Kremlin is through the Kutafya Tower, where there are toilet and cloakroom facilities. Ahead of you is the Trinity Gate, where Napoleon entered in triumph in 1812. The tower above the gate was built in 1495 but the tent roof was added almost two centuries later.
The Kremlin (the Russian word *Kreml* means fortress or citadel) is the third such structure on the present site. It occupies nearly 70 acres (28 hectares) on a hill at the confluence of the Moskva and Neglinnaya rivers (the latter now flows beneath the Alexander Garden). The walls stretch for nearly one-and-a-half miles (2.5km) and are up to 65 feet (20m) high and 21 feet

(6.5m) thick.
The first Kremlin was built shortly after 1147 by the founder of Moscow, Prince Yury Dolgoruky (Long-armed). It was much smaller than the present structure and was built of wood. A second, stone fortress was built in 1367 by Prince Dimitry Donskoi at the time of the Mongol invasions. Successive Kremlins were burnt down or destroyed until 1475, when Tsar Ivan III invited leading military architects from Italy to assist in redesigning the fortifications. This explains why the present ring of towers and walls resembles one of the great Renaissance fortresses, like the Castelvecchio in Verona. The later history of the Kremlin is equally eventful. Burnt down in 1547 and sacked by the Tatars in 1571, it was subsequently occupied for a short time by the Poles. Catherine the Great intended to replace it with a new palace complex on neoclassical lines but, fortunately, the project was abandoned. The Kremlin had an equally narrow escape in 1812 when Napoleon gave orders for it to be blown up. However, it survived, to endure a final siege by the Bolsheviks at the time of the Revolution.
On your right as you pass through the Trinity Gate is the glass-fronted **Palace of Congresses**. Opened in 1961 the auditorium, which can accommodate 6,000 people, is the setting for many of President Gorbachev's major speeches. It is also the second home of the Bolshoi opera and ballet companies, so you may well get an opportunity to have a look

around. Squeezed between the Palace and the Kremlin Walls is Communist Street (not open to the public). At the far end you can see the **Potyeshnii Palace**, where Stalin's private apartments were situated and where his wife, Nadezhda Alliluyeva, shot herself in 1932. Now turn around. The long yellow building facing you is the **Arsenal** (also closed to the public). Lined up outside are some of the French cannon captured by the forces of General Kutuzov in the campaign of 1812. Adjoining the Arsenal, at the far end, is the **Nikolskaya Tower**. The Russian heroes Minin and Pozharsky entered here to expel the Poles in 1612. Just over 300 years later the Bolsheviks stormed the Kremlin here, after a siege lasting several weeks. The large building near by with the green dome was once the **Senate** and is now the headquarters of the Soviet government. The Council of Ministers and the Central Committee of the Communist Party meet here. On the third floor are Lenin's office and private apartment, still preserved but not usually open to the public. (You can see a replica of his study in the Central Lenin Museum; see page 21.) The building nearest to the

Never fired, the Tsar's Cannon still stands in readiness

Saviour's Gate is the **Presidium** of the Supreme Soviet. The **Kremlin Theatre** is also here. To your right is the **Tsar's Cannon**—the world's largest, over 16 feet (5m) long and weighing in at nearly 36 tons (40 tonnes). Cast in 1586 for the feeble-minded Tsar Fyodor, son of Ivan the Terrible, it has never been fired, but several massive cannon balls lie ready just in case. Rising behind the cannon is the majestic **Ivan the Great Bell Tower**—for a long time, at 266 feet (81m), the tallest building in Moscow. The gigantic **Tsar's Bell**, which stands beside it, is more than 19 feet (6m) high and weighs 189 tons (192 tonnes). It was cast in 1735 but two years later a fire broke out in the Kremlin and a large section broke off when it was doused with water. The bell was never repaired.

Return to the Tsar's Cannon and you will see the **Patriarch's Palace** and the five-domed **Cathedral of the Twelve Apostles**, now the **Museum of 17th-Century Life**. These buildings date from 1645–55 and so are much later than most others in the Kremlin. On the first floor of the Palace/Museum is the Chamber of the Cross, at the time of its construction the largest room in Russia without supporting columns to hold up the roof.

The square outside is known as Cathedral Square. Stop here for a while and allow your eyes to feast on the architectural marvels which surround you. The building with the five golden domes is the **Cathedral of the Assumption** (also known as the **Dormition**). Completed in 1479

after only four years, it was designed by Aristotle Fiorovanti of Bologna. Before he embarked on the project he was sent on a tour of Russian churches by Tsar Ivan III and eventually chose the Uspensky Cathedral in Vladimir as his model. The result is a near miraculous blend of Russian and Italian styles. The largest and most important of the Kremlin churches, this is where the tsars were crowned and the patriarchs and metropolitans of the Orthodox Church laid to rest. While most of the original frescos have been lost or painted over, the overall impression is still quite breathtaking. The walls are covered in artwork of the highest quality, dating mainly from the 17th century, and there are at least two icons said to be by Dionysius (15th century). The cathedral also contains the throne of Ivan the Terrible, a magnificent piece of wood carving dating from 1551. When the French occupied Moscow in 1812 they turned the cathedral into a stable, plundering its treasures. Huge amounts of silver and gold were hauled away as booty. Much of the silver was later recovered by the Cossacks, who presented the silver and bronze chandelier which now hangs from the dome.

The **Church of the Deposition of the Robe** (1484–6) was at one time the private chapel of the patriarch. The 17th-century frescos and iconostasis (restored in the 1950s) are outstanding examples of their kind.

The building in front of you as you leave is the **Palace of the**

WHAT TO SEE – MOSCOW

Facets. Designed by the Italians Marco Ruffo and Pietro Solario in the late 15th century, it takes its name from the rusticated stone façade. The Palace, which is not open to the public, is famous for its magnificent Banqueting Hall, measuring over 598 square yards (500 sq m), where the tsars used to entertain their guests.

The **Cathedral of the Annunciation** was a private place of worship for the tsar's family and is where royal marriages and christenings took place. It was built by architects from Pskov in 1484–9. Ivan the Terrible later added four more chapels and a number of domes, before giving orders for the entire roof to be covered with gold. Forbidden by Church law to use the main entrance following his fourth marriage in 1572, he built a staircase, porch and chapel of his own, watching the services from behind a screen. The cathedral contains some of the finest artwork in the Kremlin. The frescos, dating from the 16th century, are by Theodosius, son of the famous icon painter, Dionysius. The iconostasis is hailed as the finest in Russia and includes work by Andrei Rublyov and Theophanes the Greek, once thought to have been lost.

The five-domed **Cathedral of the Archangel Michael** was built by Alevisio Novi (the Younger) in 1505–8 on the site of an earlier, 14th-century church. All the Tsars and Princes of Muscovy, from 1340 until the beginning of the 18th century, are buried here, with the exception of Boris Godunov whose body lies in Zagorsk. The frescos on the walls are mainly 17th-century. Next to the Cathedral of the Annunciation is the **Grand Kremlin Palace**. The present building with its long, yellow and white façade, dates from 1838–49 and was intended by Tsar Nicholas I to be the Imperial family's Moscow base. Nowadays, sessions of the Supreme Soviet are held here. The 200-foot (61m)-long St George's Hall, where the guests of the Tsar once danced the night away, is now used for more sober ceremonial, including the lying-in-state of Soviet rulers. The north wing of the Palace, much of it sadly hidden from view, contains the **Terem Palace**, a superb example of 17th-century architecture. Neither of these buildings is open to the public. As you leave the Grand Kremlin Palace, walk towards the Borovitskaya Tower and you will come to the **Armoury**. One of the greatest museums of its kind, it is, in effect, a storehouse of Imperial treasures accumulated from the 16th century onwards. Be sure not to miss the Fabergé eggs made for the tsar's family each Easter. Their jewel-encrusted shells open to reveal hidden treasures: a gold replica of the royal yacht, a clockwork miniature of the Siberian Express, a musical box in the shape of the Kremlin. Among the collection of royal paraphernalia are the ivory throne made for Ivan the Terrible and the fur-trimmed Crown of Monomakh, traditionally worn at coronations. Or you may be more interested in the Sevres china, the

Once a wooden fortress, the Kremlin is now a 70-acre (28-hectare) accumulation of rulers' buildings

silverware from the court of Elizabeth I, the Persian armour, the beautifully embroidered vestments and imperial robes, the carriages and sleighs. Whatever your taste, you will feel surfeited by the time you leave.

Open: the Kremlin churches and the Museum of 17th-Century Life are open every day except Thursday from 10.00 to 18.00 hrs;

the Armoury is also open every day except Thursday from 09.30 to 17.00 hrs

LENIN HILLS/LUZHNIKI

Leninskiye Gory

Known as Sparrow Hills before the Revolution, this spot offers the best panoramic view of central Moscow and is thus ideal for photographs. Take the Metro to Leninskie Gory and walk across the Luzhnikovsky Bridge. Close to the river you will see the Central Lenin Stadium, part

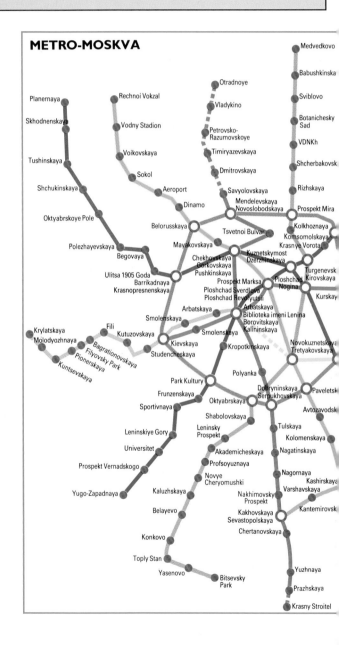

METRO-MOSKVA

Ulitsa Podbelskogo
Cherkizovskaya
Shchelkovskaya
olniki
Preobrazhenskaya Ploshchad
asnoselskaya
Pervomaiskaya
Izmailovskaya
Semyonovskaya
Izmailovsky Park
Elektrozavodskaya
Baumanskaya
Shosse Entuziastov
Novogireyevo
Chkalovskaya
Perovo
Aviamotornaya
Ploshchad Ilyicha
rksistskaya
anskaya
Proletarskaya
Vykhino
Volgogradsky Prospekt
Ryazansky Prospekt
Sharikopodshipnikovskaya
Kuzminki
Pechatniki
Tekstilshchiki
Lyublino
enino
Orekhovo
Domodedovskaya
Krasnogvardeiskaya

of the Luzhniki sports complex where the 1980 Olympics were held. Behind and to the right is the Novodevichy Convent. The skyscraper on the opposite bank belongs to Moscow State University (MGU). Completed in 1953 in Stalin's favourite Gothic or 'wedding cake' style, it is one of a set which includes the Ukraine Hotel and the Foreign Ministry building.

◆◆
MANÈGE/50 ANNIVERSARY OCTOBER SQUARE
Now the Central Exhibition Hall, the Manège was originally a military riding school. It was completed in 1825 to a design by Augustin Betancourt. Wooden girders hold up the roof, spanning 147 feet (45m), without any intermediate supports. Just across Prospekt Marksa, on either side of Herzen Street, are the old buildings of Moscow University. The building at the corner of Gorky Street is the National Hotel, one of the most fashionable hotels before the Revolution; Lenin stayed here for several days when the Soviet Government first moved from Leningrad (then Petrograd) in 1918.

◆◆◆
METRO TOUR
Intourist offers organised tours of the Metro but this is something you can do quite happily yourself. Make sure you avoid the rush hours by visiting the stations after 10.00 hrs and before 16.00 hrs, or during the evening.
The Moscow underground system is one of the great

engineering achievements of the Stalin period. The project was entrusted to two of the dictator's leading henchmen, Lazar Kaganovich and the future Soviet leader, Nikita Khrushchev. The first stretch, from Sokolniki to Park Kultury, was opened in 1935. Each station is lavishly decorated with marble, mosaic, stained glass and stainless steel. Chandeliers hang from the ceilings and sculptures and heroic murals adorn the walls. Start your tour at Ploshchad Sverdlova and try to include Komsomolskaya, Kropotkinskaya and Mayakovskaya.

◆◆
PASHKOV HOUSE/LENIN LIBRARY
Prospekt Marksa

Only a stone's throw from the Kremlin and the Alexander Garden, the Library, with more than 30 million volumes, is one of the largest in the world. The modern buildings were designed by V A Shchuko and V G Helfreich but of greater interest is the neoclassical Pashkov House, built in 1784–6 for the Governor of Siberia, P Ye Pashkov. It is now the Library Annexe.

◆◆◆
RED SQUARE
Krasnaya Ploshchad

Surprisingly, the square was given this name long before the Communists came to power; the word *krasnaya* originally meant 'beautiful' as well as 'red'. Begin your tour at the **Historical Museum** (by Prospekt Marksa Metro Station), where you must leave your bags and camera if you wish to visit the **Lenin Mausoleum**. A temporary, wooden mausoleum was erected shortly after Lenin's death in January 1924; the present structure, made from concrete and marble with a mourning band of black labradorite, was completed six years later. An awed hush descends as you enter the tomb and some Russians even cross themselves as they file past the glass sarcophagus. It is all over in a matter of seconds but the experience is unforgettable. Behind the Mausoleum and along the Kremlin wall are the graves and memorials of other honoured Communists. Stalin is interred here (his body used to lie next to Lenin's but it was secretly removed in 1961); so is the military leader, Marshal Zhukov, and the first man in space, Yuri Gagarin. Among the select group of foreigners to be honoured here is the American journalist, John Reed (author of *Ten Days that Shook the World*).

Mr Gorbachev and his Politburo colleagues mount the steps of the Mausoleum every 7 November to take the salute during the military parade which marks the anniversary of the Revolution. The changing of the guard takes place outside on the hour every hour and is well worth seeing. The soldiers march in a stately goose-step from the Saviour's Gate and complete their elaborate manoeuvre as the clock begins to chime. Heaven help them if they're late!

Immediately behind the Mausoleum is the Senate Tower,

built in 1491 by Pietro Solari. To the right is the Nikolskaya or Nicholas Tower, where a drawbridge used to span the Kremlin moat. The tower was virtually rebuilt early in the 19th century after the French tried to blow it up. On the other side of the Mausoleum is the ornate **Spasskaya** or **Saviour's Tower**. Originally designed by Solari in

Krasnaya Ploshchad means Beautiful or Red Square; the Historical Museum, where tours of the square begin, fits either description

the 15th century, the tent roof was added in 1625. Before the bells were damaged during the Revolution, they played an old Tsarist hymn; now they chime the hours and precede the time signal on Moscow Radio. Religious processions used to pass through this Gate and it was also the entrance used by tsars and foreign ambassadors. No one was allowed in on horseback and even the tsar had to remove his hat.

Opposite the Mausoleum is **GUM (State Universal Store)**, the

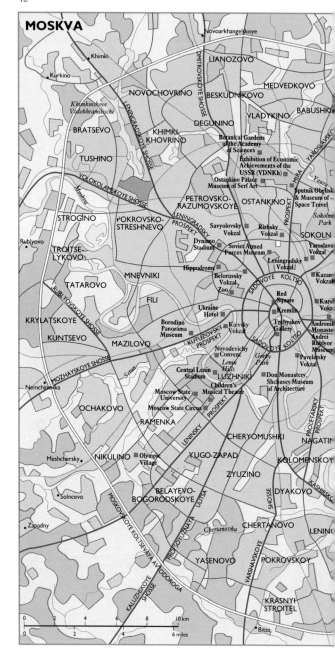

MOSKVA

Novoarkhangelskoye

Khimki

Kurkino

LIANOZOVO

MEDVEDKOVO

NOVOCHOVRINO   BESKUDNIKOVO

VLADYKINO   BABUSHKI

Khimkinskoye
Vodokhranilische

BRATSEVO   KHIMKI-   DEGUNINO
                  KHOVRINO

TUSHINO   Botanical Gardens
                 of the Academy
                 of Sciences

                 Exhibition of Economic
                 Achievements of the
                 USSR (VDNKh)   *Yauzo*

VOLOKOLAMSKOYE SHOSSE   Ostankino Palace
                                 Museum of Serf Art   Sputnik Obelisk
                                                             & Museum of
                 PETROVSKO-   OSTANKINO   Space Travel
                 RAZUMOVSKOYE

STROGINO   POKROVSKO-   *LENINGRADSKY*   *Sokoln*
                  STRESHNEVO   *PROSPEKT*   *Park*
                                      Savyolovsky   Rizhsky
Rublyovo   Vokzal   Vokzal   SOKOLN

TROITSE-   Dynamo   Soviet Armed   Yaroslavs
LYKOVO   Stadium   Forces Museum   Vokzal

                  MNEVNIKI   Hippodrome   Leningradsky
                                                        Vokzal

Moskva   Belorussky   Kazan
TATAROVO   Vokzal,   Vokzal
                  FILI   Zoo

RUBLYOVSKOYE SHOSSE   Ukraine   Red   Kurs
                                    Hotel   Square   Vokz

KRYLATSKOYE   Borodino   Kievsky   Kremlin   Andronil
                     Panorama   Vokzal   Tretyakov   Monaste
KUNTSEVO   MAZILOVO   Museum   *KUTUZOVSKY*   Gallery   Andrei
                                                    PROSPEKT   Rublyor
MOZHAYSKOYE SHOSSE   *Setun*   Novodevichy   *Gorky*   Museum
                                              Convent   *Park*   Pavelet sky
Nemchinovka   Central Lenin   Lenin   Don Monastery,   Vokzal
                     Stadium   *Hills*   Shchusev Museum
                     Moscow State   Children's   of Architecture
                     University   Musical Theatre   LUZHNIKI

                     Moscow State Circus

OCHAKOVO

RAMENKA   CHERYOMUSHKI   NAGATIN

Meshchersky   NIKULINO   Olympic   YUGO-ZAPAD   KOLOMENSKOY
                                       Village

LENINSKY PROSPEKT   ZYUZINO   DYAKOVO

Solncevo   BELAYEVO-
                  BOGORODSKOYE   *SHOSSE*   *KASHISSK*

Zapadny   *Chertanovka*   CHERTANOVO   LENING

MOSKOVSKOYE KOLTSEVAYA AVTODOROGA   YASENOVO   POKROVSKOY

PROFSOYUZNAYA ULITSA

VARSHAVSKOYE SHOSSE   KRASNYI
                               STROITEL

KALUZHSKOYE SHOSSE

0   2   4   6   8   10 km
0   2   4   6 miles

Bitsa

largest department store in the Soviet Union. Closely resembling a modern shopping mall, it was actually built in 1888–93 and was known originally as the Upper Trading Rows, a reference to some earlier market stalls destroyed during the brief French occupation of 1812. It is worth having a look inside at some point, though the crowds soon pall.

Between GUM and St Basil's Cathedral is the **Lobnoye Mesto** or **Place of the Skulls**. This was where state proclamations were read out and, as the name implies, where criminals were executed. Stenka Razin, who led one of Russia's most famous peasant revolts in 1670, was led to his execution along the street now known as Ulitsa Razina. Immediately in front of St Basil's is the **Monument to Minin and Pozharsky**. It honours the two leaders from the Time of Troubles responsible for expelling the Poles from Moscow and recapturing the Kremlin in 1612.

Originally the Cathedral of the Holy Virgin's Veil by the Moat, **St Basil's** takes its name from Basil the Blessed, the Holy Fool whose remains were interred here shortly after the church was built in 1555–60. Ivan the Terrible ordered its construction to commemorate the historic victory over the Tatars at Kazan in October 1552. The garish colour scheme dates only from the late 17th century; the cathedral was at one time painted white with gilded domes. The interior, with its maze of corridors, chapels and

twisting staircases, has to be seen to be believed. It is now a museum.

Excursions from Moscow

ZAGORSK
This is a marvellous day out, as well as an opportunity to see a little of the Russian countryside, so if you think you have the time to spare, sign up with Intourist right away.

Zagorsk is situated 44 miles (72km) northeast of Moscow. As you approach the town by road, the great Trinity Monastery of St Sergius looms into view. Founded in 1340, the fortified walls were added in the 16th century, at the same time as the stunning Cathedral of the Assumption or Dormition, with its blue domes and golden stars.

Tsar Boris Godunov's tomb stands in the shadow of Zagorsk's Cathedral of the Assumption and its dazzling blue and gold domes

The iconostasis includes a *Last Supper* by the 17th-century master, Simon Ushakov. Next to the cathedral is the tomb of Tsar Boris Godunov and his family. Zagorsk, formerly Sergievo, was for centuries one of the foremost places of pilgrimage in Russia. Prince Dimitry Donskoi came here in 1380 to ask the blessing of the founder, St Sergius, before the battle of Kulikovo. There followed the first Russian victory over the Tatars. The great saint is buried in the Church of the Holy Trinity where you can also see icons by two great medieval painters, Danil Chernyi and Andrei Rublyov.

LENINGRAD

BACKGROUND

In 1700 the Neva delta and the territory surrounding it still belonged to Sweden. Scattered about the forests and marshland were dozens of tiny settlements and fishing villages, inhabited by Finns and Russians, as well as Swedes. Trade in the region centred on the fortress of Nyenschanz, which overlooked the river bank just opposite the modern Smolny Convent. (Smolny itself was occupied by a colony of Russian tar distillers: *smola* means tar, or pitch.) Peter the Great's first attempt to gain a foothold in the region—considered vital for his Westernising ambitions—ended in a humiliating defeat at Narva; but less than three years later his army, now better disciplined and more experienced, besieged and captured Nyenschanz. Only two weeks later, on 16 May 1703, he laid the foundation stone of what was to

Peter the Great, the 'Bronze Horseman', whose ruthless ambition created the city which is now Leningrad

The tomb of Leningrad's founder, Tsar Peter I (1672–1725)

be the Peter and Paul Fortress, several miles downstream on an islet known to the local Finns as Yanni-Saari, or Hare Island. The place itself he called *Sanktpeterburg:* St Petersburg. Thousands of serfs from all over Russia, together with Swedish prisoners of war, were drafted to work on Peter's gigantic building site. There was a shortage of wheelbarrows, so the labourers carried the earth in the skirts of their clothes or in bags of rough matting. There was little food, as the area had been devastated by war and the makeshift supply system frequently broke down. Nor was there much in the way of shelter, as the wooden huts which served as barracks took years to erect in sufficient numbers. As a consequence, untold thousands died of exhaustion and disease in the service of the tsar's boundless ambition.

To populate the new capital, Peter issued decree after decree summoning precise numbers of nobles, merchants and artisans and ordering them to build their homes on designated sites, at their own expense and in conformity with his tastes and specifications. They came unwillingly, protesting at the rigours of the climate, the dreariness of the landscape and the measureless gloom of the northern winter; but they came, nonetheless. By the time of Peter's death in 1725 there were 40,000 permanent inhabitants.

Early Developments

A number of landmarks were already in place. The stone bastions of the Peter and Paul Fortress had been completed and Trezzini's Cathedral was under construction. The Admiralty was recognisable from its wooden spire, topped by a golden apple and frigate, and there was a Winter Palace (albeit a smaller, more modest version of the one you see today). There was a considerable amount of building on Vasilevsky (Basil's) Island around the Strelka—an Exchange, a Customs House and a number of wharves, as well as the huge ministerial offices or Twelve Colleges, now the University. To the south of the city, at the end of the Great Perspective Road (later Nevsky Prospekt) was the Church of the Annunciation, the earliest part of the Alexander Nevsky monastery to be completed.

As yet this amounted to little more than an urban veneer. The outskirts of the city (much of Vyborg, for example, where the Hotel Leningrad is now situated) was dense woodland, and wolves roamed the central area at night. And there were worse natural hazards. St Petersburg was regularly inundated with flood water; the tsar himself nearly drowned on one occasion. There were also devastating fires. It is not surprising, therefore, that when Peter's successor chose to return to Moscow, the nobility was only too delighted to follow suit.

From a City of Wood to a City of Stone

By mid-century, however, St Petersburg was back in favour and it underwent a transformation in the reign of Catherine the Great (1762–96). Vallin de la Mothe's Gostinny Dvor on Nevsky Prospekt dates from this period, as does the Tauride Palace and the suburban palaces at Pavlovsk and Tsarskoe Selo. The small Hermitage was built adjoining the Winter Palace, the interior of which Catherine completely refurbished in the classical style. The magnificent Anichkov Palace, overlooking the Fontanka Canal, was presented by

Leningrad is a city of open spaces: Palace Square, laid out in the 19th century

Catherine to her favourite, Prince Potemkin. The Empress also maintained a lavish court style, which was renowned throughout Europe. The Petersburg 'season' was born.

Catherine's successor, the mad Tsar Paul, built himself a new residence, the Mikhailovsky Castle, at the eastern end of the Moika and Fontanka Rivers. Terrified of assassination, this martinet of a ruler immured himself in his moated fortress. Only six weeks after he moved in, however, he was smothered in his bed by a band of military conspirators, headed by the Governor of St Petersburg, Count Pahlen.

The 19th Century

Victory over Napoleon in 1812 ushered in a new era of building activity. Some of the most impressive squares in the city were laid out to designs by Carlo Rossi: Palace Square, Arts Square and Senate Square (now Decembrists Square) are perhaps the most distinguished. Formerly a parade ground, Senate Square was the setting for an attempted coup against Tsar Nicholas I in 1825; the plotters are now regarded as the forerunners of the revolutionary

movement. Over the following decades, St
Petersburg witnessed an increasing number of
demonstrations and terrorist attacks. The first
workers' protest took place outside the Kazan
Cathedral in 1876 and, five years later, Tsar
Alexander II was killed by a bomb while driving
along the Catherine (now Griboyedov) Canal.
The Church of the Resurrection marks the spot.
By now St Petersburg was an industrial city with
a rapidly expanding workforce. As such it began
to attract young Marxist agitators such as V I
Ulyanov (Lenin), who, armed with seditious
pamphlets and leaflets, made regular forays into
the outlying factory suburbs.

City of Revolution

In time this had its effect. When Tsarist troops
fired on unarmed demonstrators in Palace
Square on 22 January 1905 (Bloody Sunday), the
workers responded with strikes and protests
which quickly spread to other industrialised
regions of Russia. The unrest was renewed in
October, culminating in a general strike, which
led to the formation of a Soviet (or council) of
Workers' Deputies. The Soviet was eventually

*Decembrists' Square,
scene of rebellion
against Tsar
Nicholas I in 1825*

suppressed, but the tsar was forced to concede Russia's first constitution.

When Germany declared war on Russia in August 1914, the name of the capital was changed to the more Russian-sounding Petrograd. Three years later, a seemingly inexorable political and economic collapse led successively to the revolutions of March and November 1917 and the triumph of Lenin's Bolshevik party. Petrograd provided the setting for most of the dramatic events of that momentous year.

In March 1918 the beleaguered Soviet government abandoned Petrograd and re-established Moscow as the capital. The ensuing civil war reduced the population of the former from $2^1/_2$ million to 720,000, many fleeing the city to escape starvation. In January 1924, following Lenin's death, Petrograd was renamed Leningrad in his honour.

The Blockade

World War II brought even greater hardship. In September 1941, Hitler's forces surrounded the city, intent on starving it into surrender. The 900 days' blockade which followed resulted in the death of more than 650,000 Leningraders, the majority of whom are buried in the Piskaryovskoye cemetery. To commemorate that terrible period, the Soviets designated Leningrad 'Hero City'.

Leningrad Today

After the war much of Leningrad and the beautiful palaces which surrounded it lay in ruins. Rebuilding began at once and restoration has been so skilful that the modern visitor can be excused for being ignorant of its post-war desolation. Today the city centre retains its 19th-century appearance, with a complete absence of skyscrapers and high-rise developments. By way of contrast, there has been a great deal of expansion in the suburbs, and Leningrad has more than doubled in size in the last 30 years. Many visitors find Leningrad more congenial than Moscow. The people appear more relaxed and approachable, while the city seems to have retained something of its Western flavour. Perhaps this is the legacy of Peter the Great.

WHAT TO SEE

Museums and Galleries

◆
CABIN OF PETER THE GREAT
Petrovskaya Naberezhnaya 6
The log cabin where Peter
supervised the construction of
the city in 1703–9. It took his
soldiers just three days to build.
The museum consists of a study
and dining room with early 18th-
century furnishings. The rigours
of the climate rather than lack of
imagination explain the outer
structure, which now protects
the cabin from the elements.
Easily combined with a visit to
the **Cruiser** *Aurora*.
Open: Wednesday to Monday
11.00 to 19.00 hrs
Closed: Tuesdays and the last
Monday of the month
Metro: Gorkovskaya

*Over 70 years ago, the Cruiser
Aurora fired the signal for the
storming of the Winter Palace. Now it
is a floating museum*

◆
CRUISER *AURORA*
*Petrogradskaya Naberezhnaya 4
(opposite the Leningrad Hotel)*
Shortly before 22.00 hrs on the
night of 7 November 1917 the
Cruiser *Aurora* (then moored
further downstream) fired a
single blank round from its bow
gun in the direction of the Winter
Palace, where the besieged
members of the Provisional
Government were still holding
out. It was the signal for the
insurgents to storm the Palace,
arrest the ministers and confirm
the Bolsheviks in power. The
Aurora was built in 1903 and saw
active service during the Russo-

Japanese War of 1904–5; one of the few ships of the Baltic Fleet, in fact, to survive the battle of Tsushima Straits, though she was badly damaged. At the time of the Revolution, the *Aurora* was in port for a refit, so her place in history is somewhat accidental. She was deliberately sunk in shallow water in 1941, later to be

The Hermitage provides an opulent setting for one of the world's greatest art collections

refloated and converted into a museum. You can visit the crew's living quarters and learn more about the ship's fascinating history from an exhibition below deck.

Open: Wednesday to Monday
11.00 to 18.00 hrs
Closed: Tuesdays
Metro: Ploschchad Lenina

DOSTOYEVSKY MUSEUM
Kuznechnyy Pereulok 5
This is the apartment where the
famous writer wrote *The
Brothers Karamazov* and where
he lived from 1878 to his death in
January 1881. You can see his
study and the drawing room
where he received visitors
during the day (he wrote
throughout the night). The
museum includes an interesting
exhibition on Dostoyevsky's life
and work.
Open: Tuesday to Sunday 10.30
to 18.30 hrs
Closed: Mondays
Metro: Vladimirskaya

HERMITAGE
Dvortsovaya Naberezhnaya 34
One of the greatest, if not *the*
greatest art gallery in the world,
the Hermitage, or State
Hermitage as it is officially
known, is also the former
residence of the Imperial family,
and provides a magnificent
setting for this unique collection.
The Winter Palace alone
contains well over 1,000 rooms,
and its main façade extends
more than a mile (1.6km). Add
the other buildings in the
Hermitage complex and you
have 12 miles (19km) of galleries
and 3 million exhibits—which is
why Intourist offers a half-day
guided tour. This is supposed to
orientate you and give you a
rough idea of the contents of the
various collections. However, it
is expensive, and you end up
somewhat breathless and
suffering more than a little from
culture fatigue. Better to arm
yourself with a plan of the gallery
and explore its delights at your
own pace. The main entrance to
the Hermitage is on the north
side of the building, overlooking
the river. If you arrive by Metro,
walk down Nevsky Prospekt as
far as Admiralty Arch, and
Palace Square is on your right.
The Hermitage consists of three
interlinked buildings: the Winter
Palace, the Small Hermitage and
the Large Hermitage. The
present **Winter Palace** (the
fourth on the existing site) was
built by Bartolomeo Rastrelli in
the baroque style for the
Empress Elizabeth in 1754–62.
Her successor, Catherine the
Great, completely redesigned
the interior, bringing it into line
with her own tastes. In 1837 the
palace was gutted by fire but
Nicholas 1 supervised its
immediate reconstruction.
The **Small Hermitage** (1764–7)
was built for Catherine the Great
as a private retreat; at one time
the only point of access was
through her personal
apartments. It became the
repository for her collection of
Dutch and Flemish masters, the
origins of the present gallery.
The **Large Hermitage** was built
in stages and took almost a
century (1770–1860) to complete.
A small bridge reminiscent of the
Bridge of Sighs in Venice spans
the Winter Canal and links the
Large Hermitage with Quarenghi's
Theatre (closed to the public).
The scale of the State Hermitage
is stupendous. Besides boasting
one of the best art collections in
the world, whole floors are

devoted to antiquities from Babylon, Assyria, China, Egypt, Greece and Rome, and there are fascinating exhibitions of coins, medals, jewellery and porcelain. But you are best advised to start with the European art, for which the gallery is most famous.

The Hermitage's outstanding collection of French painting of the 19th and 20th centuries is on the second floor of the Winter Palace's south wing. Most of the finest Impressionist and Post-Impressionist paintings exhibited here originated in the private collections of two Moscow industrialists, Shchukin and Morozov (the remainder are in the Pushkin Gallery in Moscow). Apart from works by Monet, Cézanne, Degas, Renoir and Gauguin, the Hermitage possesses 35 canvases by Matisse (Rooms 343–5) and some early masterpieces by Picasso (Rooms 346–7).

To embark on a tour of the first floor of the Winter Palace is to journey into the pre-revolutionary past. The Fore Hall, near the top of the Jordan staircase, is where the tsar's most favoured guests used to gather before dining in the sumptuous splendour of St George's Hall, which links the Palace and the Small Hermitage (Room 198). Once sated, they would drift back to the Nicholas Hall (Room 191) for the formal Imperial ball. Next-door-but-one is the Malachite Hall, where, on the night of 7/8 November 1917, Alexander Kerensky presided over his last cabinet meeting. (His colleagues were arrested in the White Dining Room and frog-marched to the Peter and Paul Fortress.) The adjoining suite of rooms was occupied by the ill-fated Nicholas II and his family, though they preferred to avoid St Petersburg after the first rumblings of revolution in 1905. Particularly impressive is the Gothic Library (Room 178). The rooms at the far end of this wing were used by Alexander II. In 1880 a revolutionary, posing as a workman, infiltrated the Palace and managed to plant a bomb underneath the tsar's dining room (Room 161). Eleven people were killed in the explosion but Alexander himself escaped. Only a year later, however, his sleigh was blown up as he was driving home and his mortally injured body was brought back to this part of the Palace, where he died.

Return now to the Jordan staircase, so called because this was the route the tsar took each 6 January for the ceremonial blessing of the River Neva. The splendid Gallery of 1812 has portraits of all the victorious generals and senior officers. This section of the Palace is known as the Great Enfilade. The Hall of St George (Room 198) was referred to earlier. This vast chamber was once the Imperial throne room and here Nicholas II inaugurated Russia's pre-revolutionary parliament, the State Duma, in 1906.

The first floor of the Large Hermitage is devoted to art of the Italian, Flemish and Spanish schools, and includes two Leonardos (Room 214), several Titians (Room 221), a Michelangelo (Room 230) and 26 Rembrandts, as well as works by Velasquez, El Greco, Rubens,

Canaletto and Tiepolo.
Open: Tuesday to Sunday 10.30 to 18.00 hrs (summer 10.00 to 18.00 hrs).
Closed: Monday

◆
HISTORY OF LENINGRAD MUSEUM
Naberezhnaya Krasnogo Flota 44
This museum concentrates on the post-revolutionary history of the city and includes a special exhibition on the 900 days in 1941–4 when Leningrad was besieged by the Germans. You can find out more about the history of St Petersburg by visiting the branch of the museum in the Peter and Paul Fortress.
Open: Mondays and Fridays 13.00 to 19.00 hrs; Tuesdays and

Sundays 11.00 to 16.00 hrs; Thursdays and Saturdays 11.00 to 17.00 hrs
Closed: Wednesdays

◆◆
LENIN MUSEUM
Ulitsa Khalturina 5/1
This former palace was built in the late 18th century for a favourite of Catherine the Great and later belonged to one of the Grand Dukes. Its sumptuous, marble interior now forms the backdrop for an exhibition tracing Lenin's development as a revolutionary. The star of the show is the armoured car from which he addressed the crowd outside the Finland Station on the night of 3 April 1917, immediately following his return to Russia.
Open: Mondays, Tuesdays, Thursday to Sunday 10.30 to 18.30 hrs
Closed: Wednesdays

Built in the 18th century, the present Winter Palace is the fourth to stand on its site

CENTRAL LENINGRAD

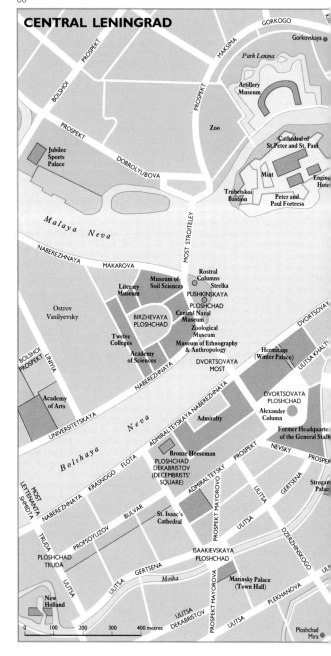

GORKOGO

Gorkovskaya

PROSPEKT

MAKSIMA

Park Lenina

Artillery
Museum

Zoo

Cathedral of
St.Peter and St. Paul

PROSPEKT

BOLSHOI

PROSPEKT

Jubilee
Sports
Palace

DOBROLYUBOVA

Mint

Engine
Hous

Trubetskoi
Bastion

Peter and
Paul Fortress

MOST STROITELEY

Malaya Neva

NABEREZHNAYA

MAKAROVA

Rostral
Columns

Strelka

Literary
Museum

Museum of
Soil Sciences

PUSHKINSKAYA
PLOSHCHAD

Ostrov
Vasilyevsky

BIRZHEVAYA
PLOSHCHAD

Central Naval
Museum

Zoological
Museum

DVORTSOVAY

Twelve
Colleges

Museum of Ethnography
& Anthropology

Academy
of Sciences

DVORTSOVAYA
MOST

Hermitage
(Winter Palace)

ULITSA KHALT

BOLSHOI
PROSPEKT

LINIYA

NABEREZHNAYA

DVORTSOVAYA
PLOSHCHAD

Academy
of Arts

UNIVERSITETSKAYA

Neva

ADMIRALTEYSKAYA NABEREZHNAYA

Admiralty

Alexander
Column

Former Headquarte
of the General Staf

Bolshaya

NABEREZHNAYA

KRASNOGO

FLOTA

Bronze Horseman

PLOSHCHAD
DEKABRISTOV
(DECEMBRISTS'
SQUARE)

NEVSKY

PROSPEK

PROSPEKT

ADMIRALTEYSKY

ULITSA

GERTSENA

Strogan
Palac

MOST
LEYTENANTA
SHMIDTA

NABEREZHNAYA

TRUDA

PROFSOYUZOV

BULVAR

St. Isaac's
Cathedral

PROSPEKT MAYOROVO

ULITSA

DZERZHINSKOGO

PLOSHCHAD
TRUDA

ULITSA

GERTSENA

ISAAKIEVSKAYA
PLOSHCHAD

Moika

PROSPEKT MAYOROVA

Marinsky Palace
(Town Hall)

PLEKHANOVA

UL

New
Holland

ULITSA
DEKABRISTOV

ULITSA

ULITSA

Ploshchad
Mira

0   100   200   300   400 metres

Mosque

October Revolution Museum

Cabin of Peter the Great

Cruiser Aurora

KUIBYSHEVA ULITSA

PETROGRADSKAYA NAB.

Bolshaya Nevka

VYBORGSKAYA

NABEREZHNAYA

LEBEDEVA ULITSA

Ploshchad Lenina

ARSENALNAYA NAB.

NABEREZHNAYA

OSHCHAD VOLYUTSII

PETROVSKAYA

N e v a

LITEINY MOST

KIROVSKY

MOST

KUTUZOVA

NABEREZHNAYA

SUVOROVSKAYA PLOSHCHAD

Lenin Museum

Summer Palace

Letny Sad (Summer Garden)

ULITSA CHAIKOVSKOGO

PROSPEKT

ULITSA CHAIKOVSKOGO

NABEREZHNAYA

KHALTURINA

Marsovo Polye

SADOVAYA

FONTANKI

Fontanka REKI

ULITSA

PESTELYA

LITEINY

ULITSA SALTYKOVA-SCHEDRINA

ULITSA

Pushkin Museum

Moika

Church of the Resurrection

Russian Museum

Engineer's Castle (Mikhail Castle)

NABEREZHNAYA

Great Puppet Theatre

ULITSA NEKRASOVA

ZHELYABOVA

Griboyedova

ULITSA

Circus

BELINSKOGO PLOSHCHAD

BELINSKOGO ULITSA

PROSPEKT

MAYAKOVSKOGO

Maly Theatre

PLOSHCHAD ISSKUSTV (ARTS SQUARE)

Philharmonic Hall

Winter Stadium

ULITSA ZHUKOVSKOGO

Kanal

Nevsky Prospekt

Armenian Church

NABEREZHNAYA

LITEINY

KAZANSKAYA PLOSHCHAD

Kazan Cathedral (Museum of Religion & Atheism)

NEVSKY

Gostinyy Dvor

PROSPEKT Anichkov Palace

Anichkov Bridge

NEVSKY

ULITSA

Gostinny Dvor, Merchant's Yard

Saltykov-Shchedrin Public Library

PLOSHCHAD OSTROVSKOGO

Pushkin Theatre

REKI

NABEREZHNAYA

PROSPEKT

Mayakovskaya

SADOVAYA

LOMONOSOVA ULITSA

VLADIMIRSKY

PROSPEKT

REKI

Fontanka

FONTANKI

Gorki Drama Theatre

FONTANKI

Vladimirskaya

The Peter and Paul Fortress has a grim and notorious past

◆◆
OCTOBER REVOLUTION MUSEUM

Ulitsa Kuibysheva 4
This imposing mansion once belonged to the great ballerina, Mathilde Kseshinskaya, a former mistress of Nicholas II. When she fled during the March Revolution, the building was taken over by the Bolsheviks, who made it their Party headquarters. It was in the white-columned drawing room that Lenin delivered his famous April Theses immediately on returning to Russia, and he frequently addressed his supporters from the balcony on the west side. The museum glories in the role played by the Bolshevik Party in the Revolution and the Civil War which followed. Photos, banners, posters and other documentation make this a worthwhile place to visit and there are sometimes film shows. (Handy for **Cabin of Peter the Great**, **Cruiser *Aurora*** and **Peter and Paul Fortress**.)
Open: Mondays and Fridays 14.00 to 19.00 hrs; Tuesdays, Wednesdays, Saturdays and Sundays 11.00 to 19.00 hrs
Closed: Thursdays
Metro: Gorkovskaya

◆◆◆
PETER AND PAUL FORTRESS

Ploshchad Revolyutsii
Situated on Zayachy or Hare Island, across the Neva from the Winter Palace, the fortress was built in 1703–10 to give

protection against the Swedes. It was, in fact, never needed for that purpose. Instead, it became one of the most notorious prisons in the Russian Empire. The Engineer's House, beyond the Petrovsky Gate, is now an architecture museum, with maps and plans showing how the city was built. At the centre of the Fortress complex is the 18th-century Cathedral of SS Peter and Paul. Replacing a wooden church, the present building was designed by Domenico Trezzini in 1713 and completed 20 years later. The golden spire, which gleams magically in the sunlight, is a landmark and used to be the tallest structure in the city. Inside the church are the tombs of most of the tsars and tsarinas from the 18th century onwards, including Peter the Great himself. Opposite the Cathedral is the Mint, which still issues commemorative coins and medals. The Trubetskoi Bastion, named like the others after one of Peter's generals, is now a museum. In former times, however, it was one of Russia's grimmest prisons—generations of revolutionaries wasted away in its cells and dungeons, though one of its earliest victims was Peter the Great's own son, beaten to death here in 1718, possibly with his father's active participation! Dostoyevsky was incarcerated here for a time; so was the demented Sergei Nechaev, who succeeded, nevertheless, in converting several of his gaolers to the revolutionary cause. (Nechaev was the inspiration for Dostoyevsky's novel *The Possessed*.) Among other notable occupants of the Trubetskoi Bastion were Leon Trotsky, imprisoned in the wake of the 1905 revolution, and Lenin's elder brother, Alexander, subsequently hanged for his role in a conspiracy to murder the Tsar. Behind the Fortress, on the mainland, is the Artillery Museum, with Lenin Park on one side and the Zoo on the other. The Fortress can easily be combined with a visit to the **Museum of the October Revolution**, which is just opposite the main entrance.
Open: Thursday to Monday 11.00 to 18.00 hrs; Tuesdays 11.00 to 16.00 hrs
Closed: Wednesdays
Metro: Gorkovskaya

PUSHKIN MUSEUM
Naberezhnaya Reki Moiki 12
Wonderfully evocative and something of a shrine for Russians, this is where the poet lived from the autumn of 1836 and where he was brought home to die following a duel with Baron d'Anthes in January 1837. The museum has recently been renovated. The rooms have period furnishings and many of Pushkin's personal possessions are on display. There is also an exhibition devoted to his life and work.
Open: Mondays and Wednesday to Sunday 11.00 to 18.00 hrs
Closed: Tuesdays

RUSSIAN MUSEUM
Inzhenernaya Ulitsa 4
Unlike the Hermitage, the Russian Museum specialises in

Russian art, mainly from the 18th century onwards. If you missed the Tretyakov Gallery in Moscow, you should certainly spend some time here if you can. There are well over 100 rooms, so it's essential to home in on the important items. Paintings by Levitsky, the 'Russian Gainsborough', are in Room 10. Rooms 67–70 contain works by the 19th-century artist, Ilya Repin, including the famous *Volga Boatmen*. In the adjoining rooms are some fine landscapes by Korovin and a friend of Chekhov's, Isaac Levitan. Don't miss the wonderful portraits of Diaghilev and Chaliapin by Leon Bakst in Room 80, or the great modern art of Larionov, Goncharova, Kandinsky and Malevich (Rooms 90–95). Room 89 has a magnificent portrait of the poetess Anna Akhmatova by Nikolai Altman.

The museum is housed in what used to be the Mikhailovsky Palace, built in 1819–25 for the Grand Duke Mikhail Pavlovich, brother of Tsars Alexander I and Nicholas I. It was converted to its present function by Nicholas II at the end of the 19th century.
Open: Wednesday to Monday 11.00 to 18.00 hrs (summer from 10.00 hrs)
Closed: Tuesdays
Metro: Nevsky Prospekt

Other Places of Interest

ALEXANDER NEVSKY MONASTERY
Situated at the far end of Nevsky Prospekt, this working monastery, founded by Peter the Great in 1713, is one of the most important in Russia. The Cathedral of the Trinity is open to the public (services are held daily at 10.00 hrs; 11.30 hrs on Sundays). Also within the monastery complex is the **Museum of Town Sculpture**, open every day except Thursday. Many of the nations' writers and musicians are buried in the cemetery here, including Dostoyevsky, Tchaikovsky and Rimsky-Korsakov.
Metro: Ploshchad Aleksandra Nevskogo

ARTS SQUARE
Ploshchad Isskustv
Off the Nevsky Prospekt near Gostinny Dvor. Both the Russian Museum and Maly Theatre are located here and the Philharmonic Hall is just around the corner in Brodsky Street. The square was laid out by Carlo Rossi in the 1830s and was intended to set off the Mikhailovsky Palace (now the museum). In the centre is a statue of Pushkin. The concert hall, formerly the Club of the Gentry, was taken over by the Russian Musical Society in 1859. Also in Arts Square is a museum devoted to the work of the modern Soviet artist I I Brodsky.

DECEMBRISTS' SQUARE
Ploshchad Dekabristov (near St Isaac's Cathedral)
The name commemorates the liberal guards officers who, in December 1825, tried unsuccessfully to stage a *coup d'état* against Tsar Nicholas I. The rebellion, which marked the beginning of the revolutionary movement, was easily put down as workmen watched in

Named after a warrior and saint who defeated the Swedes in 1240: the Alexander Nevsky Monastery

amazement from the scaffolding of St Isaac's Cathedral. Five of the conspirators were hanged and many more exiled to Siberia. Formerly a parade ground, Senate Square, as it was then called, was laid out by Carlo Rossi in the 1830s. Falconet's statue of Peter the Great, known as the 'Bronze Horseman', occupies a central position. The inscription on the base reads 'To Peter the First from Catherine the Second. MDCCLXXXII'. The statue was made famous by Pushkin in a poem of the same name. Two well-known classical buildings, the senate and the synod, occupy the western side of the square.

◆
MARS FIELD
Marsovo Polye
This huge square by the Kirov Bridge was once a military parade ground. It now commemorates those killed in the Revolution and Civil War. Occupying one side of the square are the former barracks of the Pavlovsky Regiment, whose troops were the first to mutiny during the March Revolution of 1917.

◆◆◆
NEVSKY PROSPEKT
Leningrad's majestic main street was laid out in the 1750s and was formerly known as the Great Perspective Road. It stretches fully three miles (5km), from the Admiralty to the Alexander Nevsky Monastery, and is easily reached either by Metro (Nevsky Prospekt and Gostinny Dvor lower down, Mayakovskaya and Ploshchad Vosstaniya higher up) or tram. All the major stores are located here, as is a wide variety of cafés, theatres and cinemas. Starting from the Admiralty end, the first street to the right is Gogol Street, commemorating the author of *Dead Souls* and *The Inspector General*, who lived at no 17. No 13 was the last residence of the composer,

Pushkin strikes a declamatory pose outside the Russian Museum

Tchaikovsky, who died of cholera after drinking unboiled tap water (so be warned!). The next street is Herzen Street, where you will find the Astoria Hotel. Fabergé's shop was also situated here, at no 24. Continuing along Nevsky Prospekt, the building on the right hand side with the large neon sign is the Barrikada Cinema, formerly the Club of the Nobility. Opposite, by the Moika Bridge, is the **Literature Café**, formerly the highly fashionable **Wulf et Beranger**. This is where Pushkin met his second before heading off for his fatal encounter with Baron D'Anthes. **Pushkin's house**, now a museum, is near by at 12 Moika Embankment. Cross the bridge and on your left is the Dutch church, one of a number of foreign churches on Nevsky Prospekt. The green and white building on the opposite corner is the **Stroganov Palace**, reputed to be one of the finest in Leningrad. Before the revolution the Stroganovs owned one of the best private art collections in Russia. This has now been swallowed up by the Hermitage. St Peter's Lutheran Church is at no. 22–4. Opposite is one of Leningrad's most distinguished buildings, the **Kazan Cathedral**. Completed in 1811 to a design of Voronikhin, the imposing colonnade is modelled on St Peter's in Rome. It is now the **Museum of the History of Religion and Atheism**. Kazan Square was a favourite meeting point for revolutionaries. Across the street, occupying the former premises of the Singer Sewing Machine Company, is

Dom Knigi, the city's major book store—note the distinctive globe on the roof. On your left as you cross the Kazan Bridge is the Griboyedov Canal. The large ugly building at the far end is the **Church of the Resurrection**, built on the spot where Tsar Alexander II was assassinated in 1881. No 34 Nevsky Prospekt is the Melodiya record shop. A little further up on the right hand side is the long façade of **Gostinny Dvor**, or **Merchant's Yard**. Completed in the reign of Catherine the Great, it is now Leningrad's premier department store, the equivalent of GUM in Moscow, and just as crowded. The street running off to your left is Brodsky Street, where both the Philharmonic Hall and the Yevropeiskaya Hotel (Hôtel de l'Europe) are situated. **Arts Square** is at the far end. Continue along Nevsky Prospekt and on your left you will see the blue and white Armenian church, followed by the Passazh Department Store. A little higher up, at no. 52, is **Yeliseev's** food store, which still retains something of its pre-revolutionary opulence. The next major intersection, just beyond Gostinny Dvor, is Sadovaya Street. Cross it and the building on your right is the **Saltykov-Shchedrin Public Library**, a favourite haunt of, among others, Tolstoy and Lenin. **Ostrovsky Square**, designed by Carlo Rossi in the 1820s, is named after the 19th-century playwright, A N Ostrovsky. The elegant yellow building is the **Pushkin Theatre**, where Gogol's *Government Inspector* was first performed. In the garden outside is a statue of Catherine the Great. On the far side of the square is the **Anichkov Palace**, which once belonged to Catherine the Great's favourite, Prince Potemkin. The **Anichkov Bridge**, which spans the Fontanka River, is famous for the four rearing horses which decorate each corner. The Fontanka is probably the most suitable point to conclude your tour of Nevsky Prospekt. If you wish to carry on, you will eventually come to Ploshchad Vosstaniya (Uprising Square), where the Moscow Railway Station is situated. From here you can take the Metro back into town or, alternatively, proceed to the Alexander Nevsky Monastery, but this is a good walk.

◆◆◆
PALACE SQUARE AND THE ADMIRALTY

Dvortsovaya Ploshchad
This splendid square, with the green and white **Winter Palace** as its focal point, was laid out in its present form by Rossi in the 1820s. On the far side, opposite the Palace, is the former Main Staff building of the Russian Army, actually two buildings linked by a gigantic arch. At the centre of the square is the **Alexander Column**, made from red granite and erected to commemorate Russia's defeat of Napoleon in 1812. Military parades were held here and the tsar would cross the square on horseback, sometimes accompanied by visiting heads of state, to review his troops. In January 1905 Palace Square was the scene of a massacre, when

soldiers opened fire on unarmed demonstrators gathering to present a petition to the tsar. The incident, known in Russian history as Bloody Sunday, sparked off the revolution of that year. Twelve years later, Bolshevik forces began their attack on the Winter Palace from this point, though there was no frontal assault of the kind portrayed by Eisenstein in the film *October*.

The fine classical building immediately to the west of the square is the **Admiralty**. Designed by Zakharov at the beginning of the 19th century, it is instantly recognisable by its gilded spire, crowned by a weather-vane in the shape of a sailing ship. The Admiralty stands on the site of Peter the Great's first shipyard, constructed in 1704.

◆◆
ST ISAAC'S CATHEDRAL AND SQUARE

Isaakiyevskaya Ploshchad
There has been a church on this site since 1710 but the present building dates from the early 19th century. It was finally opened in 1858. The vast interior, capable of accommodating 14,000 worshippers, is lavishly, if rather tastelessly, decorated. Note the iconostasis, with its malachite and lazurite columns. The cathedral is now a museum but the exhibition which traces its history is in Russian only. Don't leave without climbing the dome which offers a magnificent panoramic view of the city. Tickets are on sale inside the building but photography,

unfortunately, is not permitted.
Open: Thursday to Monday,
11.00 to 18.00 hrs; Tuesday, 11.00
to 16.00 hrs
Closed: Wednesdays
The most important building in St
Isaac's Square lies on the south
side, across the Siniy Most, or
Blue Bridge. This is the **Marinsky
Palace**, where the Tsar's Council
of Ministers used to meet before

*Crowds follow the broad sweep of
Leningrad's Nevsky Prospekt*

the Revolution. In 1917 it was
taken over by the Provisional
Government. Nowadays it
serves as Leningrad's Town Hall.

◆
SMOLNY INSTITUTE
Situated next door to the
colourful Smolny Convent, the
Smolny Institute was originally a
school for daughters of the
nobility. In 1917 it became the
premises of the Petrograd Soviet
and of the Bolshevik Central

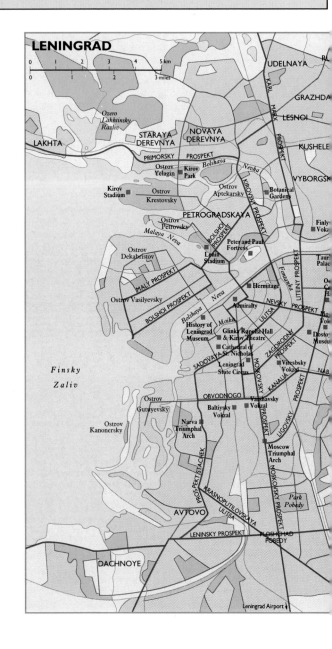

LENINGRAD

Committee. It was to Smolny that
Lenin came in disguise to
oversee the Communist seizure
of power. His government
continued to meet here until
March 1918, when it moved to
Moscow. In December 1934 the
Leningrad party boss, Sergei
Kirov, was assassinated
here—the event which
preluded Stalin's purges.
Open: daily, except Sunday.
Excursions by reservation

◆
VASILYEVSKY ISLAND
A short walk across Palace
Bridge, Vasilyevsky or Basil's
Island was to have been the
centre of Peter the Great's new
city. Instead it became a
residential district and was
known in the 19th century as the
German quarter. From the
Strelka (arrow head) there is a
magnificent view of the city. The
Rostral Columns, which rise from
the square, mark the site of the
original port and once served as
lighthouses. The white-
columned building, once the
Stock Exchange, is now the
Central Naval Museum. Next
door is the Zoological Museum.
Further round, on the Malaya
Neva Embankment, is the
Literary Museum, formerly the
Customs House. On the other
side of the Strelka, beyond the
Zoology Museum, are the
**Museum of Ethnography and
Anthropology** and the **Academy
of Sciences**, founded by Peter
the Great in 1725.

River Tours
Though the rivers and canals of
Leningrad are iced over for
much of the winter, boat travel is

a highly enjoyable way to see
the city in summer. There are
several alternatives. The
cheapest ride takes you from
Naberezhnaya Krasnovo Flota
(Red Fleet Embankment, near
the statue of the Bronze
Horseman) to the **Smolny
Institute**. This will give you an
excellent view of the Strelka, the
Hermitage, the Peter and Paul
Fortress, the Summer Gardens
and the area around Smolny
itself.
Alternatively, you can pick up a
boat at the **Anichkov Bridge**
(nearest Metro—Gostinny Dvor,

*The magnificent blue and white
Cathedral of the Smolny Convent*

Mayakovskaya) and tour the
inland waterways and canals. In
summer months, Intourist will
provide an English-speaking
guide, but this is much more
expensive than going under your
own steam (the cost of the ride
alone will seem very good value
at the moment, providing you
can pay in roubles).

Excursions Outside Leningrad
Intourist offers a tour of the
various summer residences of

the tsars, and this is well worth subscribing to if you are staying in Leningrad for any length of time.

The two most interesting are **Pushkin** (formerly Tsarskoe Selo—Tsar's village) and **Petrodvorets** (Peter's Palace). All the palaces were thoroughly looted before being blown up by the Germans during the war, but each one has now been painstakingly restored.

◆◆
PAVLOVSK

Only a few miles from Pushkin, Pavlovsk is usually part of the same Intourist package. If you are travelling independently, take the no 280 bus from Pushkin; or the train from Vitebsk station in Leningrad, then bus no 283 or 493.

This palace, a little matter of 1,300 acres (526 hectares), was a gift from Catherine the Great to her son Paul. It was designed along classical lines by Scotsman Charles Cameron and completed in 1786. The Halls of Peace and War on the first floor are among the most attractive in the palace. The grounds are magnificent.

Open: Saturday to Thursday, 11.00 to 18.00 hrs
Closed: Fridays and first Monday of each month

◆◆
PETRODVORETS

Petrodvorets is on the southern shore of the Gulf of Finland, 18 miles (29 km) from Leningrad. The fastest route in the summer is along the Malaya Neva, by hydrofoil (May to September). Otherwise take the train from the Baltic station in Leningrad (Naberezhnaya Obvodnovo Kanala, Metro: Baltiskaya), then buses 350, 351 or 352 from Novy Petergof Station.

Petrodvorets, known in Tsarist times as Peterhof, was first occupied by Peter the Great while he was overseeing work on the great fortress of Kronstadt, near by. A visit to Versailles in 1717 transformed his relatively modest ambitions. The small palace of Montplaisir, which overlooks the sea, was completed by the time of Peter's death in 1725. The Great Palace, on the other hand, was virtually rebuilt by Rastrelli and only completed in 1754. The *pièce de resistance* is the Great Cascade, a glorious display of fountains, terraces and waterfalls descending to the sea.
Open: Tuesday to Sunday, 11.00 to 18.00 hrs
Closed: Mondays and the last day of each month

◆◆
PUSHKIN

If you want to make your own way to Pushkin, take the train from Leningrad's Vitebsk Station (Zagorodny Prospekt, Metro—Pushkinskaya) to

WHAT TO SEE – LENINGRAD

Dyetskoye Selo, then buses 371 or 382, which go directly to the palaces. Alternatively, Intourist will take you there by coach and will supply an English-speaking guide.

Pushkin, formerly Tsarskoe Selo, is situated about 15 miles (25km) south of Leningrad. It is named after the great Russian poet, who went to school here and owned a *dacha* (summer home) in the vicinity. In Tsarist times, Pushkin was a fashionable haunt of the aristocracy, who were anxious to be near the imperial family and to escape the noxious air and oppressive climate of the capital. After the Revolution of 1905, Nicholas II and his family lived here more or less permanently and spent several months under house arrest following the March Revolution of 1917. Pushkin was overrun by the Germans in 1941; when they left three years later the palaces were devastated.

Waterfalls, terraces and gardens form a majestic symmetry in the Great Palace of Petrodvorets

The Catherine Palace was built in baroque style by the great Italian architect, Bartolomeo Rastrelli, in the 1750s (he later went on to design the Winter Palace). It replaced an earlier building, commissioned by the Empress Elizabeth and named after her mother, the wife of Peter the Great. Elizabeth's successor, Catherine the Great, subsequently called in another architect, the Scotsman, Charles Cameron, to redesign the interior in the classical style to which she was partial. The decoration is magnificent throughout. The walls of the Picture Hall, designed by Rastrelli, are covered with more than 130 paintings, most of them originals. Exquisite stucco bas-reliefs adorn the Green Dining Room, and silks with Chinese motifs give the Chinese Blue Drawing Room its name. Adjacent to the palace are the baths, sumptuously decorated in agate and jasper. There is a great deal to see outside. The Ulitsa Vasenko leads from the side of the palace, past the Pushkin statue to the yellow and white Alexander palace, residence of Nicholas II from 1905 to 1917. His children played in the pond nearby. The Catherine Park, which is a delight to stroll in during summer, reveals the essential frivolousness of the age. There is a Turkish bath made to resemble a mosque, a Chinese pavilion and a cemetery where Catherine buried her favourite pet dogs.

Open: Wednesday to Monday 10.00 to 18.00 hrs
Closed: Tuesdays and the last day of each month

PEACE AND QUIET

Wildlife and Countryside in Moscow and Leningrad
by Paul Sterry

The Soviet Union's geography ranges from snow-capped mountain peaks to deserts and from inland seas to the tundra of the Arctic coast. Although visitors to Moscow and Leningrad can only hope to experience a fraction of this variety, many interesting habitats lie within a short distance of these cities. Visitors with an interest in natural history may feel a little frustrated. At the time of writing, trips to nature reserves cannot be made without prior arrangement with Intourist and even then many sites are effectively placed 'out of bounds' by bureaucratic problems. If you wish to visit a specific site, contact Intourist well before you leave home, but be prepared for disappointment. Alternatively, you could join one of the few specific natural history tours organised by companies based in the west.

Without prior arrangements, the best opportunities for observing wildlife are had by joining excursions to the countryside, rural villages or stately parks; as long as you are away from the urban environment there will be something to see. By referring to the habitats covered later in the text and recognising the type in which you find yourself, you can get a good idea of what to look for.

In and Around Moscow

Most visitors to Moscow come to marvel at the splendour of its architecture and to experience a different culture, but the city's parks make a pleasant and relaxing contrast to the buildings. Although they lack the species diversity of woodlands in the surrounding countryside,

The grey and black hooded crow

sites such as Gorky Park or Izamilovo Park sometimes harbour a surprising variety of birds.

The Botanic Gardens of the Academy of Sciences at Ostankino have patches of semi-natural mixed woodland, along with a wide variety of plant species from elsewhere in the Soviet Union. Hooded crows and starlings are resident, but during migration time in spring and autumn, birds such as barred warblers, willow warblers, greenish warblers and red-breasted flycatchers may turn up.

Because Moscow lies well inland, the climate is distinctly continental, with hot summers and cold winters. The severity of the winter, which drives many species of birds south to warmer climates, freezes the Moskva River. However, in summer, a boat trip is a good way to see the sights. Parties of swifts scream overhead and the river sometimes hosts black-headed gulls and small groups of marsh terns.

Leningrad

Leningrad's position on the coast ensures that it generally has a milder climate than Moscow, although this still does not prevent the Neva River from freezing during the winter months. Parks and gardens are plentiful, and many serve as a haven for a variety of birds as well as weary tourists.

Close to the city centre, the Summer Gardens, Lenin Park, which contains the Zoological Gardens, Kirov Park and Park Pobedy harbours trees and shrubs attractive to wildlife, while further afield, Primorsky Park Pobedy on Kresovsky Island and the gardens in Pushkin also merit a visit. Butterflies are attracted to ornamental flowers, and resident hooded crows are sometimes joined by summer visitors such as robins, thrushes and pied, spotted or red-breasted flycatchers.

Excursions to the Island of Kizhi on Lake Onega should give you the opportunity to see waterbirds such as grebes and ducks; and a trip to the Kirov Islands or a cruise in the Gulf of Finland may offer views of seals or seabirds such as great black-backed gulls, Caspian terns, black guillemots, eiders, cormorants or divers.

The Russian Steppe

To the south of Moscow there once lay a great band of temperate grassland known as the steppes, which stretched from the Polish border to China. Although much of the natural vegetation has disappeared under the plough, pockets of steppe vegetation still persist in nature reserves, and many of the less intensively farmed regions retain some of their former wildlife features.

Sheep's fescue, feather grass and wormwood are the dominant plants but in spring, tulips, grape hyacinths and crocuses add splashes of colour to the sea of grass. In autumn, spiked speedwell appears and the songs of grasshoppers and bush crickets fill the air. Birds of the steppes include pallid harriers, rose-coloured starlings, several

You are not likely to see the saiga antelope outside nature reserves

species of larks and waders and the immense great bustard. Mammals such as sousliks and marmots live in underground burrows and are quite widespread, while the once endangered saiga antelope is still more or less restricted to reserves.

Outstanding areas of steppe can be seen in the Askania-Nova Reserve near the Black Sea and the Central Black-Earth (Tsentralno-Chernozomny) Reserve at Kursk.

Broad-Leaved Woodlands
Moscow lies in a transition zone between the hardy coniferous forests of northern Russia and the scrub and steppe habitat to the south. The typical natural

vegetation of the region around the capital is mixed forest comprising scattered evergreen trees and a wide range of broad-leaved, deciduous species such as oak, beech, lime and birch. Although much of the native woodland has been cleared in the immediate vicinity of Moscow, mature parks and gardens in the suburbs often retain many woodland species and large tracts of prime forest can be found farther afield from the capital.

During the winter months the woodlands may appear bleak and austere, often giving the impression of being lifeless. Many of the birds have migrated to more favourable climates, while most of the invertebrates and some of the mammals pass the cold months in states of dormancy or torpor. However,

PEACE AND QUIET

wild boar, deer and foxes still have to forage for food and great-spotted woodpeckers, lesser-spotted woodpeckers and flocks of tits forage for insects hidden among the twigs and bark.

Those smaller birds that do remain during the winter months generally move around in roving flocks, so visitors should patiently look and listen for their presence: initially there will be nothing in sight; then, all of a sudden, the trees will be full of birds as a flock moves through. After dark, tawny owls hunt for small mammals and their presence can be detected by the familiar 'kewick' call.

In spring, the woodland floor bursts into life with patches of wood sorrel, primroses and orchids playing host to a variety of insects, including butterflies such as orange tip, speckled wood and brimstone. By late summer, the shade cast by the leaf canopy is too dense to allow much light through to the ground below. Most ground-dwelling flowers therefore make use of light available in spring.

Spring also heralds the arrival of migrant birds such as pied, spotted and red-breasted flycatchers, chiffchaffs, blackcaps, redstarts and cuckoos; on their arrival, they add to the chorus of bird song from the resident species. At

Silvery streaks of taiga trees: birch, poplar and pine

ground level, mice and voles scurry among the fallen leaves and red squirrels are more conspicuous at this time of year than at other seasons.

The Taiga

Taiga is the Russian name given to the great belt of coniferous forest that dominates the northern latitudes of the country. It stretches all the way from the Baltic coast to the Sea of Okhotsk. Spruce and fir trees dominate these woodlands, and these evergreen trees can tolerate some of the harshest winter weather. Not surprisingly, the taiga has been a rich source of timber for building and firewood, the evidence for this being most noticeable around towns and cities. However, in areas cleared of conifers, birch is quick to colonise and a mosaic woodland soon forms.

The shade cast by dense stands of conifers is such that the ground flora is comparatively poor, although mosses, liverworts and ferns often thrive in the damp, still air. Their growth is particularly rich in clearings and rides when flowering plants such as bilberries, wintergreens and coralroot orchids sometimes appear. Fungi appear in the autumn and are more noticeable in birch woodland than under conifers. Many different shapes and colours can be found, including species of *Boletus* and fly agarics.

The birdlife of the taiga is noticeably different from that of the broad-leaved woodland. Beautifully marked hazelhens nest and feed inconspicuously on the woodland floor, while black woodpeckers and white-backed woodpeckers excavate their own hole in the trunk of a tree. Ural owls and great-grey owls, on the other hand, use the fork of a tree or sometimes occupy an abandoned crow's nest. Both species of owl are large and will take quarry as large as a capercaillie or a hare. Thrushes are also well represented in the taiga: blackbirds, redwings and fieldfares build neat nests of twigs and mosses in the forks of trees. Crossbills are widespread and small flocks form outside the breeding season. As their name suggests, the tips of the bill are crossed and are ideally suited to prising out the seeds from pine cones.

Many of the taiga's mammals have beautifully warm coats, which help them endure the winters. Regrettably, these also make them targets for the fur-trade and species like fox, wolf and sable are justifiably wary of man. The forests also harbour elk, or moose, and despite their massive size these huge creatures are surprisingly quiet and unobtrusive.

Tundra

The tundra is the most northerly vegetated zone in the Soviet Union, occupying an area beyond the forested taiga. To the north lies the frozen Arctic, a land of ice flows and shattered rock. Because of the northerly latitude it occupies, the tundra is necessarily difficult to reach, but the Kola peninsula is the most accessible area from Leningrad. With the exception of prostrate

PEACE AND QUIET

forms of juniper, dwarf birch and dwarf willow, this is a treeless landscape, but one which is nevertheless botanically rich. Although blanketed by ice and snow in winter, mosses, clubmosses and lichens are abundant, and during the brief summer mountain avens, cowberry, crowberry, Arctic poppy, moss campion and saxifrages add colourful variety.

The marshy ground is home to millions of midges and also to large numbers of birds. Waders such as dotterel, spotted redshank, greenshank, golden plover, broad-billed sandpiper, red-necked phalarope and Temminck's stint and numerous wildfowl nest close to water, while ptarmigan, lapland buntings and snowy owls prefer more broken ground. The latter species feeds mainly on lemmings and Arctic voles, which, in some years, can be abundant.

The Baltic Coast

After visiting the sights of Moscow and Leningrad, a trip to the Baltic Coast or a cruise along the Gulf of Finland can make a refreshing change. The sea air is invigorating and the wide range of maritime species of bird, which are not found inland, adds variety to a trip to Russia. During the summer months, undisturbed stretches of coast hold a number of breeding birds. Black guillemots and eider ducks nest on rocky coasts but spend a considerable amount of time feeding on the sea. Black guillemots catch fish, while eiders prefer mussels and

other shellfish. Red-throated divers also fish on the open sea but nest beside inland pools. Together with black-throated divers, grebes and seaduck, their numbers build up during spring and autumn migration. Gulls are also very much a feature of the coast, the numbers and the variety of species changing with the seasons. Black-headed, common and little gulls are summer visitors, while many herring and great black-backed gulls remain throughout the year. Flocks should be checked in winter for glaucous gulls, adults of which are immediately recognisable by their large size and pure white wings.

Belovezhskaya Pushcha Reserve

Belovezhskaya Pushcha lies on the western border of Russia and is contiguous with the world-famous Bialowieza Reserve in Poland. The primeval forests that comprise this remarkable area are among the most unspoilt in Europe, and are home to an amazing variety of plants and animals. The reserve provides an insight into what much of Europe must have looked like thousands of years ago.

Compared to many areas in Europe, mammals are well represented in the reserve with wild boar, foxes, wolves, polecats, pine martens, dormice and harvest mice all being present. Most famous of all, however, is the population of European bison, which have been saved from the brink of extinction.

Broad-leaved trees, such as oak, hornbeam and alder,

predominate in Belovezhskaya and, in turn, support breeding birds such as pied flycatchers, golden orioles, black storks, honey buzzards, lesser spotted eagles and several species of woodpeckers. Marshy ground is home to tree frogs, common frogs, common toads, green toads and birds such as great snipe, ruff, great reed warblers and river warblers.

Pondering his close shave ... one of the European bison, rescued from extinction and living at the Belovezhskaya Pushcha Reserve

The Oka Reserve

The Oka Reserve lies in the Ryazan district, less than 100 miles (160km) to the east of Moscow, and is the capital's most accessible reserve. It is an area of varied habitats comprising mixed woodland, and elements of steppe, taiga and marshland vegetation, with the River Oka as its centrepiece.

European bison, which were introduced from Poland, and aurochs now breed here, and the woodlands harbour red squirrels, roe deer, pine martens

PEACE AND QUIET

and numerous small mammals. White-tailed eagles, ospreys, black kites, kingfishers, otters and introduced beavers are found in the vicinity of the river and marshes, which support large numbers of frogs, toads and newts. The marshland vegetation is rich and colourful and includes irises, fritillaries and marsh orchids, while in the more boggy areas sundews, bog myrtles and bilberries grow. Several species of woodpecker, including the immense black woodpecker, excavate nest holes in the larger tree trunks, and black storks and honey buzzards build nests of twigs and branches. In early spring warblers and flycatchers arrive and sing loudly to claim a territory.

The Darwin Reserve and Rybinsk Reservoir

Two hundred miles (320km) to the north of Moscow lies the immense Rybinsk Reservoir, which is situated on the transition zone between Russia's broad-leaved deciduous forests and the coniferous taiga further north. The Darwin Reserve, which borders the northern shores of the lake, mainly comprises large tracts of taiga with spruce and pine predominating, but variety is added to the area by marshes and bogs.

Open marshland is home to cranes which, despite their size, are extremely wary creatures ideally suited to the expansive terrain. Flowers such as cottongrass and sundew flourish in the marshlands, which also provide ideal nesting grounds for teal, mallards, shovelers,

curlew and wood sandpipers. All species keep a wary eye open for white-tailed eagles, which nest in the forests and prey upon unsuspecting birds and mammals.

Wolverines, wolves and brown bears live in the forest but are retiring species, usually only seen by chance, as are the nesting Ural and great-grey owls.

Travelling Farther Afield

Although Moscow and Leningrad themselves can be exciting enough, trips can occasionally be made farther afield to visit some of the more spectacular regions of mountains, deserts and inland seas. These normally need to be planned well in advance, and often mean joining an organised tour.

Lake Baikal is one of the more distant destinations, lying near the border with China in the foothills of the Transbaikalian Mountains. The lake has been land-locked for so long that many of its species are unique and found nowhere else in the world. It can even claim its own species of seal.

Nearer to Moscow, the Black Sea and Caspian Sea (the largest inland sea) offer aquatic life on a grand scale. The Caspian also has its own species of seal, and both have unique species of fish and huge breeding colonies of wetland birds around their margins. Less easy to visit but unsurpassed in their mountainous splendour are the Caucasus Mountains, the Tien Shan Mountains and the Pamir Mountains of Uzbekistan.

Russian markets are worth exploring, for the characters if not for the food itself!

FOOD AND DRINK

As you have probably learnt from your newspapers, there are serious shortages of even basic foodstuffs in the Soviet Union at the moment and the situation is unlikely to improve in the near future. Even hotel food has deteriorated recently, though you will not go hungry. Since devaluation, eating out in restaurants offers good value for money and, strange as it may seem, the quality of the food is often better than in the hotels. You may also find a rouble self-service cafeteria in the hotel which will offer a reasonable choice of hot and cold dishes for as little as 4.50 roubles. If you are a vegetarian, inform your tour representative immediately on arrival at the hotel.

Breakfast (*zavtrak*): you will probably take this in your hotel. It will normally consist of a slice of cheese or salami followed by a boiled or fried egg. Both courses will be accompanied by generous helpings of bread, butter and jam. If you're lucky, you may even be offered pancakes (*bliny*) and sour cream. There will be fruit juice to drink (often undrinkable), but if you're a coffee addict, prepare to be disappointed. Coffee is

FOOD AND DRINK

astronomically expensive and even in hotels you can expect only one miserly cup with your meal. Tea, on the other hand, is in plentiful supply and you can usually find some milk.

Lunch (*obyed*): the main meal of the day in the Soviet Union. You will be served a selection of *hors d'oeuvres* (zakuski; **закуски**), then soup, a meat or fish dish and a dessert. Expect quantity rather than quality. There will be little in the way of fresh fruit and vegetables and you will see enough coleslaw and dills to last

a lifetime! Since the dessert, too, will be unappetising, why not eat among Russians instead? That way, you will also have more time for sight-seeing.

If you're hungry, you might like to try a cafeteria (*stolovaya*; **столовая**). Here you can buy fairly simple fare like macaroni and meatballs for less than a rouble and, while the quality is decidedly 'greasy spoon', it's an experience not to be missed. Simply point to what you want,

A food and drink kiosk in Moscow

then pay at the cash desk before returning for your food. There are stolovayas all over Moscow. If they sound too down-market for you, or you don't think your stomach can take institutionalised food Soviet-style, try a café (*kafe*; кафе) instead. You can buy a three-course meal at one of these establishments for just four or five roubles (see **Restaurants**, pages 86–8).

In Moscow, a Pizza Hut is due to open on Ulitsa Gorkovo, and you will also be able to have a McDonalds; the world's biggest branch is now on Pushkin Square.

If you don't want to sit down, then stop off at one of the numerous stalls specialising in one of the following: kebabs (*shashlichnaya*; шашлычная); pancakes (*blinaya*; блиная); pies (*pirozhkovaya*; пирожковая); sausages (*sosiskaya*; сосиская); or stuffed dumplings (*pyelmennaya*; пелменная).

Dinner (*oozhen*): your hotel will provide a three-course meal in the evenings (hors d'oeuvre, meat or fish, dessert) but take at least one night off to sample one of the wide selection of restaurants. The best ones are in great demand, so you would be well advised to book a table through Intourist. The alternative is to arrive at 18.00 hrs—or even earlier—and join the queue. Try walking straight up to the door and showing the commissionaire your hotel card. This will usually get you in ahead of turn but don't bank on it.

When you eat out in the Soviet Union, be prepared to relax and make an evening of it like the locals. Service is slow and there will be a long wait between courses, but you won't find the Russians complaining. Sit back and enjoy the music (there will probably be a band or cabaret) or join in the dancing. Some sample dishes are listed below. The menu may not be translated, so you might have to point or take pot luck—accept this as part of the fun. You will notice a big jump in price between cafés and restaurants. A meal in a good, state-run restaurant will usually cost in the region of 30—50 roubles with wine. If the bill is much higher than this, you can always opt to pay in hard currency, negotiating a price to your advantage. If you are dining out at a co-operative, expect to pay much more. When you come to pay the bill (*shchot*; счет) check your change carefully and leave a small tip in foreign currency. Most restaurants close at about midnight but there are some—the Slaviansky Bazaar in Moscow, for example—which sometimes stay open until 01.00 or 02.00 hrs.

Appetizers
caviar (*ikra*; икра)
pancakes with caviar (*bliny s'ikroi*; блины с икрой)
pancakes with sour cream (*bliny so smetanoi*; блины со сметаной)
pickled mushrooms (*marinovaniye griby*; мaринованые грибы)
smoked salmon (*kopchonaya syomga*; копуеная семга)

Dessert
apple pie (*yablochny pirog*; яблочный пирог)

ice cream (*morozhenoye*; мороженое)
rum baba (*romovaya baba*; ромовая баба)

Drinks

beer (*pivo*; пиво): sold in bottles and often of good quality.
brandy (*konyak*; коньяк): Armenian and Azerbaijani brands are highly recommended, though the latter is expensive.
kvass (квас): a slightly alcoholic drink fermented from rye bread, popular in the summer.
vodka (водка): usually sold in measures of 100 grams. Common brands are Stolichnaya and Moskovskaya.
water (*voda*; вода): drink bottled mineral water, not tap water.
wine (*vino*; вино): the best Soviet wines come from Georgia, Moldavia or the Crimea. Wines from Bulgaria are also acceptable. Try Tsinandali (dry white) or Mukuzani (dry red). For those with a sweet palate, try the wines from the Caucasus and the Crimea like the muscatel, Red Star (*Krasnaya zviezda*). You will also find champagne (*shampanskoye*) on most menus. Do not expect Moet et Chandon! Russian sparkling wines tend to be very sweet but very cheap (eg, 8 roubles a bottle) and lie quite easily on the stomach. There is a Georgian sparkling dry white wine called Chkhaveri, which can be recommended.

Fish

fried pike-perch (*sudak fri*; судак фри)
herring (*syeld*; сельдь)
salmon (*syomga*; семга)
sturgeon in tomato sauce (*osetrina po-russki*; осетрина по-русски)
trout (*foryel*; форель)

Meat

beef Stroganoff (ьеф-строганов)
chicken Kiev (*kotlety po-kievski*; котлеты по-киевски)
duck with apples (*utka s'yablokami*; утка с яблоками)
grilled steak (*bifshteks*; бифштекс)
kebabs (*shashlik*; шашлык)
pies (with a variety of fillings) (*pirogi*; пироги)
pilau rice with mutton (*ploff iz baraniny*; плов из баранины)
roast pork with plums (*zharkoye iz svininy so slivami*; жаркое из свинины со сливами)

Soups

beetroot, cabbage and meat (*borshch*; Борш)
cabbage and meat (*shchi*; ши)
cold vegetable (*okroshka*; окрошка)
meat or fish soup, flavoured with cucumber, tomatoes, olives, capers, lemon and sour cream (*solianka*; солянка)

Moscow Restaurants

Aragvi, Ulitsa Gorkogo 6. Georgian cuisine: Sulguni cheese, spiced meat soup (*kharcho*), roast sturgeon (*osetrina na vertelye*) and chicken tabaka. Georgian wines: Tsinandali, Mukuzani, Kakhetia.
Ararat, Ulitsa Neglinnaya 4. Armeninan dishes: *solyanka*, Yerevan *bozbash*, trout, *shashlik* and deep fried meat pies (*cheburek*).
Baku, Ulitsa Gorkogo 24, Azerbaijan dishes, including more than 20 kinds of pilau

(*ploff*), sour milk and meat soup
(*dovta*), grilled sausage (*lyulya-
kebab*), stuffed vine leaves
(*golubtsky*) and roast lamb with
pomegranates (*nakurma*).
Wines: Matrassa, Shamkhor.
National Hotel (Russky Zal),
Ulitsa Gorkogo 1. High quality
Russian cuisine. Try the *borshch*
and the *blinys*.
Slaviansky Bazaar, Ulitsa 25
Oktobrya 13. Russian style menu
in what was Chekhov's favourite
restaurant. Noisy.
Sofia, Ulitsa Gorkogo 32. Russian
and Bulgarian cuisine.

Snacks on the banks of the Neva

Uzbekistan, Ulitsa Neglinnaya
29. Specialities include meat and
noodle soup (*lagman*), Scotch
eggs (*tkhum-dulma*) and roast
mutton ribs (*baranina kopeka*).
Uzbek wines.

Co-operative Restaurants
An experiment in private
enterprise, launched as part of
the Gorbachev revolution in
1987. Co-ops buy at market, not
subsidised prices, so the food is
expensive but of generally
better quality than the State
restaurants. They tend not to be
very central.
Atrium, Leninsky Prospekt 44.

FOOD AND DRINK

Kolkhida, Sadovaya-Samotyochnaya 6. Georgian food in a pleasant setting.

Ulitsa Kropotkinskaya 36. The first co-operative restaurant in the Soviet Union. Standard Russian cuisine.

A new Jewish restaurant called **U Josefa** has opened recently. Ask Intourist for details.

Cafés

Arktika, Ulitsa Gorkogo 4.

Artisticheskoye, Proyezd Khudozhestvennogo Teatra 6.

Govori, Ulitsa Gorkogo (near Intourist Hotel).

Ogni Moskvy, in the Moscow Hotel, Prospekt Marksa 2.

Bars

If you're adventurous, try the **Yama** (Pit), a *pivnoi* or beer bar on the corner of Ulitsa Pushkinskaya and Stoleshnikov Pereulok. You'll see a queue forming outside at about 17.30 hrs or even earlier. Leave your coat in the cloakroom and you'll be given a helping of shrimps and black bread. Beer is served from automatic dispensers and is surprisingly good but the surroundings, to be honest, are squalid. Closes at about 20.30 hrs. Hard currency bars are to be found in the following hotels: Intourist, Cosmos, National and Rossia. Closing time varies from midnight to 04.00 hrs.

Leningrad

Restaurants

Leningrad boasts a number of high quality restaurants. The following are recommended:

Baku, Ulitsa Sadovaya 12. Good, spicy Azerbjaijani cuisine. *Hors d'oeuvres* (*zakuski*) include fish in walnut sauce and mild pickled peppers. *Satsivi* and *basturma* also recommended. Reservations required.

Kavkazky, Nevsky Prospekt 25. Georgian cooking. Try the *kharcho* soup, the *khinkkali* (peppered mutton dumplings) and the bread, which is delicious.

Neva, Nevsky Prospekt 46. Try the *shchi* and any of the large variety of fish dishes. Downstairs is the Sever Café, which is famous for its pastries.

Petrovsky Zal, Hotel Leningrad, Vyborskaya Naberezhnaya 5/2. Traditional Russian food, served to the accompaniment of a folk ensemble.

Sadko, Nevsky Prospekt/Ulitsa Brodskogo. Attached to the Yevropeiskaya Hotel. Traditional Russian cuisine with good live entertainment. Very popular, so make sure you book.

Sovyetski, Prospekt Lermontova 43. A hotel restaurant serving no-nonsense traditional Russian food.

Cafés

For a daytime snack or cheaper evening meal try one of the following:

Avtomat, Nevsky Prospekt 45. Self-service.

Druzhba, Nevsky Prospekt 15.

Fregat, Vasilevsky Island, Bolshoi Prospekt 39/14. Cheap and cheerful, best in the evenings.

As in Moscow, there are numerous *bliny* bars and ice-cream parlours. There is a *bliny* bar, called **Blinnaya**, on Nevsky Prospekt 74, while ice cream is served at **Ogonyok**, Nevsky Prospekt 24.

SHOPPING

Moscow

Beriozka Shops

You'll find these at airports and in hotels. In Moscow the largest and best stocked ones are in the **Rossia Hotel** and at **Kutuzovsky Prospekt 9**, near the Ukraine Hotel. Beriozkas accept only foreign currency, travellers' cheques and the major Western credit cards. Prices are marked in roubles and the cashier then converts them into hard currency equivalents.

The Beriozkas are almost empty at the moment. This is because, since currency devaluation, you can buy your souvenirs much more cheaply in Russian shops, even if this sometimes means queueing. Items on sale include glassware, china, furs, jewellery, perfumes, toys and Western as well as Soviet brands of drinks and cigarettes.

Some ideas for presents:
Vodka: the prices may seem steep but look for quality brands, which are not usually on sale in the shops of the West.

Colourful costumes sported by ranks of Russian dolls. Souvenirs are generally cheaper in Russian than in Beriozka shops

SHOPPING

Palekh boxes: hand-painted and lacquered by local craftsmen, some from the village of Palekh near Moscow. These make very attractive gifts.

Matrioshka: the famous Russian nesting dolls.

Records and cassettes: very cheap and perfectly playable but of inferior technical quality to those available in the West. Go for recordings of Russian music.

Balalaikas: traditional Russian stringed instrument, variously priced.

Posters: these make ideal gifts but you will get a better selection at **Dom Knigi** or **Isskustvo** (see below).

Opening hours 10.00–14.00 hrs and 15.00–19.00 hrs (18.00 hrs on Saturday).

There is a special Beriozka book shop on **Ulitsa Kropotkinskaya 31** which stocks Russian books seldom found elsewhere in Moscow, as well as art books and records. Although you pay in hard currency, prices are still relatively cheap.

Vneshtorgbank Gold Shop, Ulitsa Pushkina 9, is good for gold, silver and jewellery; and **Estée Lauder** have recently opened a shop on Ulitsa Gorkogo.

Soviet Shops

Don't be shy about having a look around, even if you don't want to buy anything. Prices are always marked in roubles. To make a purchase, choose what you want and ask or signal to the assistant to write down the price, then queue at a cash desk (*kassa*; касса) to pay. Finally, return to the counter with your receipt and collect your purchase.

Opening hours approximately 09.00–19.00 hrs (some department stores open at 10.00 hrs but stay open until 21.00 hrs). Closed Sundays (except some larger stores in the city centre).

The main shopping streets are Ulitsa Gorkogo, Prospekt Kalinina and Ulitsa Arbat. Recommended shops:

Central Army Store, Prospekt Kalinina, before Arbat turn-off. This is where to buy your army belts, bags, badges, insignia, etc. What you are allowed to buy seems nowadays to depend on the attitude of the assistant who serves you. You are not normally allowed to buy epaulets.

Dom Knigi (House of Books), Prospekt Kalinina 26. Largest bookshop in Moscow. Also sells posters at about 10 kopeks a time.

Dyetski Mir (Children's World), Prospekt Marksa 2. Children's clothing, toys, etc. Worth a look, but as the quality of Soviet toys leaves something to be desired, you'll probably end up buying presents for children at the Beriozka.

Gastronom No 1 Moscow's most famous food store. Note the opulent décor, which dates back to pre-revolutionary times.

GUM, Krasnaya Ploshchad (Red Square) 3. Department store/ shopping mall. There is now a credit card only shop here, selling Western and luxury items.

Kommissionyi Magazin (Commission Shop), Ulitsa Arbat 32. Antiques. Bear in mind, however, that valuable items (including books) may carry an export duty of 100 per cent.

The huge GUM shopping mall

Leningrad

Beriozka Shops

Nevsky Prospekt 9. The largest in Leningrad, selling everything from cameras to toys, fur hats to vodka and cigarettes. There is another Beriozka nearby, at **Ulitsa Gertsena 26**. You will also find branches in the larger Intourist hotels like the Sovietskaya, but the range of goods is generally more limited. Beriozka opening hours: 10.00–14.00 hrs and 15.00–19.00 hrs (18.00 hrs on Saturdays).

SHOPPING

Soviet Shops

Opening hours: approximately
09.00–19.00 hrs (some
department stores open at
10.00 hrs but stay open until
21.00 hrs). Closed Sundays.
Leningrad's main shopping
street is Nevsky Prospekt.
Recommended shops:

Central Army Store, high up on
Nevsky Prospekt, about 10
minutes' walk beyond Gostinny
Dvor. Soviet army belts, bags,
badges, insignia, etc. You are
not normally allowed to buy
epaulets.

Dom Knigi, no 28. Leningrad's
premier book shop, once the
premises of the Singer Sewing
Machine Company. Buy your
posters here, also.

Gostinny Dvor, no 35. This
elegant building, known as the
Merchants Yard; dates back to
1785 and the reign of Catherine
the Great. Today it is a rambling
department store on the GUM
model. Worth a look around, as it
will give you an insight into the
lot of the Soviet consumer.

Komissionnyi Magazin
(Commission Shop), no 52.
Antiques. Valuable items,
including books, may carry an
export duty of 100 per cent.

Melodiya, no 34. Record store.

Passazh, no 48. Another large
department store.

Yeliseev, no 56. Leningrad's
main food store. Yeliseev owned
the shop before the Revolution
and the name has stuck, at least
in popular memory.

Markets

There is a large fruit and
vegetable market in **Kuznechnyy
Pereulok** (Metro-
Vladimirskaya). This is where
the well-heeled Soviet citizen
buys his or her groceries. The
quality and variety far exceeds
what is usually on offer in State
stores but so do the prices!

An indoor market in Leningrad

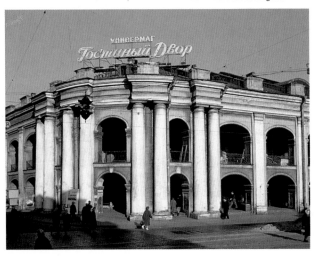

The elegant, shining curve of the Cosmos, one of Moscow's major Intourist hotels, built by the French for the 1980 Olympics

ACCOMMODATION

Whether you are travelling to the Soviet Union on a package tour or making your own arrangements, you will have precious little say in where you stay. Intourist make all the arrangements for you and you will only know the name of your hotel on arrival. This unsatisfactory state of affairs is likely to continue for some time to come, since the dearth of first class accommodation has worsened following the recent,

post-*glasnost* tourist boom. There are three classes of accommodation: luxury, first class and tourist class. The cost of a room in luxury class accommodation will be in the region of 120–150 roubles per night; in first class, expect to pay between 80 and 95 roubles in the better quality hotels; elsewhere, from 50 roubles upwards, depending on the season. (Tourist class is used mainly for student/youth groups, etc, and is not always available.) Package tourists can expect first class facilities, comprising single or double room with bath or shower, toilet and telephone. Most modern hotel rooms also have a radio. At the moment,

ACCOMMODATION

however, even a single room cannot be guaranteed and some tourists may end up in cabin accommodation aboard a liner! If this is your fate, your single room supplement will be refunded *in the Soviet Union*.

Registration

When you arrive, you will be asked to hand over your passport and visa and to fill in a registration form. You can ask for your travel documents back after about 48 hours; otherwise, they will be returned to you just before you leave. In exchange, you will be given a key card, with your floor and room number printed on it. Keep this with you at all times. Whenever you leave the hotel, hand your key to the floor attendant (*dezhurnaya*) —she will give it back to you when you return. You will also need to show your card to the doorman as you come in. The

The world's biggest hotel: the Rossia, which can take 6,000 guests

dezhurnaya is the person to complain to about broken light bulbs, lack of toilet paper, or other inconveniences. She will also make you tea (for a price), book your phone calls home and see to your laundry. So it's worth keeping on the right side of her. If she has been helpful during your stay, you might like to make her a small gift of some tights, perfume or Western cigarettes. She is sure to appreciate the gesture.

Moscow

All the major Intourist Hotels you're likely to stay in (Rossia, National, Intourist, Cosmos, Ukraine, Belgrade—the Metropole is closed at the time of writing for refurbishment) —have the following facilities: café(s), restaurant(s), hard currency bar(s), hairdresser, post office, laundry service and excursion bureau. The Intourist and Cosmos hotels both have swimming pools.

Belgrade, Smolenskaya 5 (tel: 248 6692; Metro: Arbatskaya).

Cosmos, Prospekt Mira, 150 (tel: 217 0786; Metro: VDNKh). Perhaps the best modern hotel, built by the French for the Moscow Olympics in 1980. Accommodates 3,000. Soulless; far out from central Moscow.

Intourist, Ulitsa Gorkogo 3–5 (tel: 203 4080; Metro: Prospekt Marksa).

Metropole, Prospekt Marksa (tel: 225 6673). Designed by a British architect, W Walcott. When it's restored it will be Moscow's premier hotel and will be well worth a look around, even if you're not lucky enough to be staying there yourself.

National, Prospekt Marksa 14, near Red Square (tel: 203 6539; Metro: Prospekt Marksa). Lenin stayed here for a while when the Soviet Government moved to Moscow from Petrograd (Leningrad) early in 1918.

Rossia, Ulitsa Razina 6 (tel: 298 5500), which can accommodate 6,000 people, is the largest hotel in the world. You will find it just behind Red Square—you can't miss it! (Metro: Ploshchad Nogina).

Savoy Hotel, Ulitsa Rozhdestvenka. Recently reopened as a Soviet-Finnish joint venture. Another top grade establishment.

Ukraine, Kutuzovsky Prospekt, 2 (tel: 243 3030; Metro: Kutuzovskaya). There are a number of overspill hotels, most, if not all of which should be of a more than adequate standard. Two fairly typical examples are the **Sovietskaya**, on Prospekt Leningradskogo 32 (tel: 250 2342; Metro: Dinamo), and the rather bleak-looking **Sevastopol**, Bolshaya Yushunskaya Ulitsa 1 (tel: 119 6450; Metro: Kakhovskaya). Many tourists from Eastern Europe stay here.

Leningrad

Western tourists are likely to be assigned to one or other of the following hotels, all of which have first class facilities:

Astoria, Ulitsa Gertsena 39. Centrally situated, with an atmosphere reminiscent of old St Petersburg (closed for refur-bishment at the time of writing).

Leningrad, Vyborgskaya Naberezhnaya 5/2 (Metro: Ploshchad Lenina). A modern, rather luxurious hotel with excellent facilities. Opposite the Cruiser *Aurora*.

ACCOMMODATION

Moskva, Ploshchad Aleksandra Nevskogo 2 (Metro: Ploshchad Aleksandra Nevskogo). A modern hotel, situated near the famous Nevsky Monastery. Acceptable standards but remote from the city centre.

Pribaltiyskaya, Ulitsa Korablestroitelei 14 (Metro: Primorskaya). Another modern hotel, Swedish-built and close to the port (its address is Shipbuilders' Street). Too large and impersonal for some tastes but facilities include six bars/

Looming over the Moskva (Moscow) River, the stately Ukraine Hotel has a distinctive outline

snack bars, saunas, swimming pool, bowling-alley and souvenir shop, so there are compensations.

Pulkovskaya, Ploshchad Pobedy 1. New, Finnish-built hotel with all mod. cons. Highly spoken of.

Yevropeiskaya, Ulitsa Brodskogo 1/7. Another hotel of pre-revolutionary vintage, currently being renovated.

CULTURE, ENTERTAINMENT, NIGHTLIFE

First the bad news: there is no nightlife in the Soviet Union, at least in the Western sense of the term. There aren't any night clubs and, if you want to have a drink and chat after about 23.00 or 23.30 hrs, you will have to resort to the hard currency bars of the major hotels: Intourist, National, Rossia and Cosmos. These close at various times from midnight to 04.00 hrs. If you do decide to drink late, don't

The promise of excitement: a poster for the Moscow State Circus

forget that the Metro begins running down at about 00.30 hrs. The best way to let your hair down in the Soviet Union is to spend the evening in one of the city's livelier restaurants (see pages 86–8). This is where you are most likely to see ordinary Russians enjoying themselves and you'll find their sense of fun and *joie de vivre* infectious. Restaurants generally stay open until midnight and you can take as long as you like over your meal. Many have dance bands and/or a floor show, so you will be fully entertained. However, the better ones are in great demand so, to make sure of a table, book through Intourist.

Moscow

Cinemas
All films are in Russian and even
foreign language films are
dubbed in Russian without
subtitles. Showings are not
continuous and you are entitled
to see one film only. There is no
admission after the start of a
performance.
Cosmos, Prospekt Mira 109
Metropole, Prospekt Marksa 1
Oktyabr, Prospekt Kalinina 42
There is also a cinema in the
Rossia Hotel.

Circus
The world famous **Moscow State
Circus** performs at Prospekt
Vernadskovo, 7. Nowadays, the
packaging is as much variety
show as traditional circus and
many foreigners find the acts
disappointing. During the
summer there are tent circuses
in **Gorky Park** and at **VDNKh**
(Exhibition of Economic
Achievements).

*It's worth making the effort to see a
production at the Kirov Theatre in
Leningrad: it has been associated
with many great names*

Jazz

Try the **Sinyaya Ptitsa** (Blue Bird) on Ulitsa Chekhova but be prepared for long queues.

Opera, Theatre and Ballet

You certainly will not want to leave the Soviet Union without sampling at least one of the cultural offerings for which the country is justly famous. Tickets for most productions are hard to come by, so as soon as you have settled in, find out what's on from your tour company or Intourist representative and book through them. (Theatre tickets are also sold at kiosks, but they will invariably have sold out if the production's at all worth seeing.) Nowadays, you can expect to pay something more akin to the going *Western* rate for a performance, rather than the face value of the tickets (three to five roubles). Before you go off at the deep end, remember that, being a foreigner, you stand a much greater chance of getting to a performance than the average Soviet citizen—as you will appreciate when you see the forlorn figures milling about the theatre forecourt in search of unwanted tickets (culture is taken seriously here).

Most visitors want to spend an evening at the **Bolshoi Theatre** on Ploshchad Sverdlova. If the ballet or opera companies are not performing here, the alternative venue is the **Palace of Congresses** within the Kremlin (entrance through the Kutafya Gate).

Rock/Pop

Rock music has finally emerged from the closet in the Soviet Union, though to Western eyes and ears it still seems a little behind the times. Concerts are held in **Gorky Park** and there is also a **Rock Laboratory** and a **Rock Club** in Moscow. Groups to look out for include Cruiz, Black Coffee (heavy metal), Svuki Mu and Bravo.

Symphony Concerts and Recitals

These take place at the **Tchaikovsky Hall** on Ploshchad Mayakovskovo, another building in serious need of repair (Metro—Mayakovskaya). Concerts also take place at the **Conservatoire**, Ulitsa Gertsena 13 (Metro—Kalininskaya) and at a number of smaller halls. Look out for performances by the State Symphony Orchestra, the Piatnitsky Folk Choir, the Moscow Virtuosi under Vladimir Spivakov and the Beethoven Quartet.

Theatre

The **Moscow Art Theatre** (MKhAT), famous for its associations with Chekhov and Stanislavsky, is at Proyezd Khudozhestvennovo Teatra 3 and Ulitsa Moskvila 3. Other theatres include the **Maly**, on Ploshchad Sverdlova and at Ulitsa Bolshaya Ordynka; the **Moscow Drama Theatre**, known sometimes as Malaya Bronnaya from its location on Ulitsa Malaya Bronnaya; and the **Taganka Theatre**, Ulitsa Chkalova. There are also a number of new experimental theatres, some of which already have a reputation for excellence. Look out for Anatoly Vasilyev's **School of Dramatic Art** and Oleg Tabakov's **Studio Theatre**. (Check with Intourist for further information.)

CULTURE, ENTERTAINMENT, NIGHTLIFE

Leningrad

Nightlife, in the Western sense of the term, does not exist in Leningrad, any more than in Moscow. Restaurants generally close at about 23.30 hrs, the foreign currency bars of hotels anywhere between midnight and 04.00 hrs. Those at the **Leningrad Hotel**, Pirogovskaya Naberezhnaya 5/2, stay open latest. The foreign currency bar in the **Sadko** restaurant closes at 02.00 hrs.

Chaika, Ulitsa Brodskogo. This German sponsored foreign currency bar, managed by OPC-Siemens, is the place to go if you are missing your home comforts.

Cinemas

All films are in Russian and showings are at specific times. There are cinemas all over Leningrad but the main theatres include:

Avrora, Nevsky Prospekt 60.
Barrikada, Nevsky Prospekt 15.
Primorsky, Kirovsky Prospekt 42.
Saturn, Ulitsa Sadovaya 27.

Circus

The Leningrad State Circus is at Naberezhnaya Reki Fontanki 3. Summer performances take place on Moskovsky Prospekt.

Concerts

Glinka Kapella Hall, Naberezhnaya Reki Moiki 20. The Glinka choir was founded by Peter the Great in 1713. Its standards are excellent and concerts are well worth attending.

Leningrad Philharmonia Concert Hall, Ulitsa Brodskogo 2 (Metro—Nevsky Prospekt). Now referred to as the Shostakovich Philharmonia, in honour of the great Soviet composer who was born here in 1906. Orchestra of world renown.

October Concert Hall, Ligovsky Prospekt 6 (Metro—Ploshchad Vosstaniya).

Small Hall of the Philharmonia, Nevsky Prospekt 30.

Opera, Theatre and Ballet

Leningrad has a vibrant and varied cultural life which is well worth exploring. The main theatres are:

Kirov Theatre of Opera and Ballet, Teatralnaya Ploshchad 2. Known before the Revolution as the Marinsky. Some of Tchaikovsky's most famous ballets (including *Sleeping Beauty* and *The Nutcracker*) were premiered here and the great Russian bass, Chaliapin, regularly trod the boards. The Kirov company has been much praised recently, so if Intourist offer you tickets, snap them up!

Gorky Drama Theatre, Naberezhnaya Reki Fontanki 65.

Maly Theatre of Opera and Ballet, Ploshchad Isskustv 1 (Metro—Nevsky Prospekt). The name means 'small' but the Maly actually seats 1,200.

Pushkin Theatre, Ploshchad Ostrovskogo 2 (Metro—Gostinny Dvor).

Rock/Pop

There is a Rock Club in Leningrad at Ulitsa Rubinshteina 13 (off Nevsky Prospekt). The best-known Leningrad bands are Avtograf and Televizor. Popular Mekanix is an experimental band, playing a cross between rock and classical avant-garde.

Winter in Russia is bitterly cold, but it can also be spectacularly beautiful: the snow-capped Trinity Monastery of St Sergius in Zagorsk

WEATHER AND WHEN TO GO

Moscow

You can enjoy Moscow any time of year. The weather is wonderfully invigorating in winter but also *very* cold (temperatures well below freezing are by no means uncommon any time from December to February). Snow begins to fall during November, with the thaw beginning in March, so if you dislike rain and slush avoid this period. (You will be surprised at how efficiently snow is cleared from the streets, incidentally.) By way of contrast,

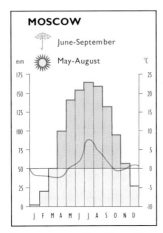

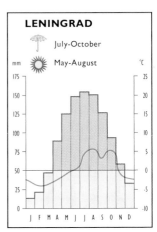

the summer months of June, July and August tend to be very hot, with temperatures rising to 30°–35°C (85°–95°F) in August.

What to wear

Winter: a warm winter coat covering the upper part of your legs is essential; likewise, a pair of warm trousers (jeans are not ideal in the depths of winter). You will also need a Russian-style fur hat or *shlyapka*, complete with ear muffs (a bobble or ski hat will not be enough). If you can not find something suitable at home, then buy one at the nearest Beriozka at the first opportunity. (If you speak Russian, you will be able to pick up a hat more cheaply at the **TsUM Department Store**, Ulitsa Petrovka 2, close by the Bolshoi Theatre). Make sure also that you have a well-lined pair of gloves, a scarf and a sturdy pair of shoes or boots with skid-resistant soles. You do *not* need to worry about feeling cold indoors; Soviet central heating

systems are remarkably efficient.

Summer: dress as you would in any West European country, but remember to pack a raincoat and umbrella. Take your swimming things, too.

Leningrad

Generally, the climate is similar to Moscow. Leningrad tends to be a few degrees warmer during winter but it often *feels* colder, because of the icy winds which whip across the Neva. In summer, on the other hand, the climate is just about ideal— warm but not too hot. For tourists lucky enough to be in the city during the latter part of June, the famous White Nights are a magical bonus.

HOW TO BE A LOCAL

The Russians are an open, generous and emotional people and on the whole you will find them far less suspicious of foreigners than they used to be. They appreciate politeness, so try to learn the words for 'please', 'thank you' and 'excuse me' before you arrive. You may well arouse curiosity on the Metro, particularly if you are in a group. Do not be surprised if you are stared at from time to time; older Russians find Western dress and behaviour somewhat extrovert. They are at their best in the more relaxed surroundings of bars and restaurants and you may well be invited over to their table or asked to dance. They will be offended if you turn them down. If you happen to be travelling on the Red Arrow (the night train which runs between Moscow and Leningrad) you may find yourself sharing a sleeping compartment with a

Night becomes day during Leningrad's White Nights; night-time views such as this one of the River Moika can be disconcertingly bright!

Russian couple! In these situations, formal introductions and handshakes are the norm. If you are a young person, you may like to visit the official friendship organisation, *Dom Druzhby* (House of Friendship), situated on Prospekt Kalinina. Here you can meet young Russians over a drink of tea. However, they will be a very select breed of Russian—members of Komsomol, the Communist youth organisation, who have learnt their English at special schools. You may find the company at a Soviet rock concert more congenial: find out from Intourist what's on at the Green Theatre in Moscow's Gorky Park, or at the Moscow Rock Club. You will meet students there and, if you are lucky, you may be invited back to their homes or to their rooms on campus, an experience not to be missed. In

case such an opportunity does come your way, bring some Western pop magazines over with you—they will be much appreciated.

PERSONAL PRIORITIES

Work on the assumption that you will be unable to find any of the following items in the Soviet Union and that it is therefore essential to bring your own more than adequate supplies with you: nappies, creams and everything for baby; tampons or sanitary towels, male and female contraceptives, deodorants, toilet paper, etc.

A note on clothing: older Soviet men and women can be a little starchy regarding dress so if you want to avoid being stared at on the Metro or in the street, leave behind excessively alluring gear, *eg* very short skirts, tight jeans, etc. And remember that the bars of the larger Western hotels are favourite pick-up points for Soviet prostitutes so women are best advised not to drink alone.

CHILDREN

Moscow

Soviet cities are not particularly well suited to the needs and interests of children. However, here are some ideas you might like to try:

The Circus: book through Intourist. If you are unlucky and the world famous Moscow State Circus is on tour, the reserve team will be playing in Gorky Park.

Ice shows: the Moscow Ice Ballet performs at the Lenin Stadium, Lenin Hills. Check with Intourist for details.

The Zoo: Gruzinskaya Bolshaya Ulitsa, 1 (Metro: Krasnopresnenskaya). Opening hours: 10.00–17.00 hrs daily.

Toys: be careful about buying toys made in the Soviet Union (unless from the Beriozkas)— they may be unsafe. However, you may like to take your children to have a look at the Russian toys at the Dyetski Mir (Children's World) Department Store on 2 Prospekt Marksa.

Swimming, skating, etc: see Sport.

Theatre for children: the Central Puppet Theatre at 3 Sadovaya-Samotyochnaya is well worth a visit; likewise, the Central Children's Theatre, 2/7 Ploshchad Sverdlova and the Children's Musical Theatre, Prospekt Vernadskovo. If you are interested in mime, try the Mime Theatre at Izmailovsky Boulevard, 41. For times of performance and other details, see Intourist.

Parks: there are several major Moscow Parks, with the usual recreational facilities (cafés, restaurants and so on). Gorky Park (Metro:Park Kultury), Sokolniki Park (Metro: Sokolniki) and Izmailovo Park (Metro: Izmailovskaya) are worth visiting. Gorky Park, the most popular with Muscovites, has an amusement area with boating lake, fun fair, fountains and open-air theatre, among other delights. Or you can watch the skating in winter.

River cruises: if you are in Moscow between June and September/October, why not take your children for a cruise on the Moscow river? Departs from the jetty near the Kiev Railway

Station (Metro—Kievskaya).
Troika rides: available at
VDNKh (USSR Exhibition of
Soviet Economic Achievements:
Metro—VDNKh) from 25
December to 8 March. Book
through Intourist.
Food and drink: try the
pancakes (*bliny*) on sale in the
shop just across the road from
the Zoo, or the Sputnik ice-
cream parlour on Ulitsa Gorkovo
(near the Intourist Hotel). The
collective name for these
establishments is *Morozhenoe*
(**мороженое**).

*A Matrioshka, or nesting doll, can
provide one 'mother' or a whole
family, according to your wishes*

CHILDREN

Leningrad

The Leningrad Circus, Fontanka
Naberezhnaya 3. A must if you
have been unable to get to the
Moscow State Circus. Book
through Intourist as soon as you
arrive.
The Zoo, Park Lenina 1, at the far
end of Prospekt Maksima
Gorkovo. Open daily at 10.00 hrs.
Closing times vary according to
season.
Toys: there is a toy department
in the handicraft shop at Nevsky
Prospekt 51.
Swimming, skating, etc: see **Sport.**
Theatre for children: the Great
Puppet Theatre, Ulitsa

A trip on the Leningrad Harbour
Ferry is a treat for children and adults
alike, and makes a change from
trudging the streets

Nekrasova 3 is worth a visit.
Parks: the Kirov Park on Yelagin
Island has the best recreational
facilities in Leningrad. Or you
might try the Park Pobedy on
Moskovsky Prospekt (Metro:
Park Pobedy).
River cruises: available in the
summer. Boats leave from the
pier by the Winter Palace and
from the Anichkov Bridge on
Nevsky Prospekt. Ask Intourist
for details.

Food and drink: there is a café specially for children on Nevsky Prospekt 42. Otherwise, try one of the pancake shops (*bliny*) or ice-cream parlours (*morozhenoye*) which are dotted about the city.

TIGHT BUDGET

Unless you are visiting the Soviet Union on a youth or student exchange, the package tour is still the best value for money you are likely to find. Buy your lunch from a stand-up snack bar or cafeteria and you will only be spending a rouble or two. Whenever possible, wander around on your own and avoid the tour guides—that way you will save money *and* learn a lot more about what makes the Russians tick. If your feet get tired pounding the pavement, jump on a bus or take the Metro; it's only five kopeks a ride. Museum charges are also very reasonable, once you have dispensed with the guided tour, so take your travel guide with you instead. When buying presents, have a look round the local stores before diving into the Beriozka. Records, art books, posters, etc are excellent value for money, even if there is not much to choose from. Or see the local crafts on display at a peasant market.

SPECIAL EVENTS

Moscow
There are major parades on May Day, 1 May; Victory Day, 9 May and Anniversary of the Revolution, 7 November. Celebrations during the latter include gymnastic and firework displays and dancing. Mikhail Gorbachev and the other Soviet leaders take to the reviewing stand on top of the Lenin Mausoleum in Red Square. During the **Russian Winter Festival**, 25 December to 5 January, which includes the celebration of New Year, there is a programme of concerts, theatre and other cultural happenings.
A similar festival takes place from 5 to 13 May (**Moscow Stars Festival**).

Leningrad
Major parades: May Day, 1 May; Victory Day, 9 May and Anniversary of the Revolution, 7 November. The last-named is particularly important in Leningrad, of course, because this is where the Revolution actually took place. Try to get as near to the Neva as possible and you should catch a glimpse of the Baltic Fleet as it makes its way up the river towards the Winter Palace. Illuminations at night.
Russian Winter Festival: 25 December to 5 January, includes New Year celebrations. There is an ambitious programme of concerts, theatrical performances and other events.
Farewell to Russian Winter: 19 February to 5 March, activities include folklore festival.
Leningrad White Nights: 21 to 29 June, another major festival.

SPORT

Moscow
Cross-country skiing: available at several locations in or just outside Moscow. Ask an Intourist

representative for details.

Horse racing and cycling: these take place at the Hippodrome, Ulitsa Begovaya 22. There is horse racing on Saturday and Sunday afternoons.

Horse riding: lessons may be arranged through Intourist.

Ice hockey: the two Moscow football clubs, Dynamo and Central Army Club, play ice hockey in winter.

Ice skating: there are skating rinks in winter at the Gorky and Sokolniki Parks (open 10.00 to 22.00 hrs). Ask your Intourist desk about hiring skates, or enquire about them at Sokolniki Park.

Soccer: the Soviet football season runs from spring to autumn. Teams usually play on Saturday afternoons. Tickets may be obtained from the Intourist desk at your hotel. The major venues are **Dynamo Stadium**, 36 Leningradsky Prospekt and **Army Palace of Sports**, 39 Leningradsky Prospekt. Important matches (including internationals) may also take place at the **Lenin Stadium/Palace of Sports** at Luzhniki (Lenin Hills).

Swimming: there is an open air, heated swimming pool, open year round from 07.00 to 23.00 hrs, at Kropotkinskaya Naberezhnaya, 37. There are also swimming pools at several hotels, including Intourist, Cosmos, Rossia and Mezhdunarodnaya.

In the summer you can go swimming at the beach in Seryebryany Bor, but don't forget to check with Intourist if you intend leaving the confines of Moscow.

Tennis: there are outdoor courts reserved for foreigners at Luzhniki, Lenin Hills.

Leningrad

Cycling: Vyborgskoye Chaussee 14; Engels Prospekt 81.

Cross-country skiing: there is a centre at Olgino on the Gulf of Finland, but remember that you must inform Intourist before leaving the confines of Leningrad.

Skating: there is a rink open during the summer at 15 Liniya 2 and an open air skating rink for children at the Central Recreation Park, Tavrichesky Sad.

Soccer, hockey and other spectator sports: the major venues are **Kirov Stadium**, Krestovsky Island, **Lenin Stadium**, Krestovsky Island, **Jubilee Sports Palace**, Ulitsa Zhdanovskaya 2 and **Winter Stadium**, Manezhnaya Ploshchad 6. For tickets and further information, see the Intourist desk at your hotel.

Swimming: there is a small swimming pool in the **Pribaltiskaya Hotel**, Ulitsa Korablestroitelei 14 (Metro—Primorskaya). Alternatively, try one of the following: Nevsky Prospekt, 22–5, Ulitsa Bolshaya Raznochinnaya 20, Prospekt Dinamo 44 (Krestovsky Ostrov), Novocherkassky Prospekt 5a, Ulitsa Dekabristov, 38, Ulitsa Litovskaya/Lesnoi Prospekt.

Outdoor pools: Prospekt Dinamo 2, Ulitsa Olginskaya 6, Naberezhnaya Bolshoi Nevi 24. There are beaches at Park Pobedy and the Central Recreation Park.

DIRECTORY

Contents

A view of Red Square in Moscow

DIRECTORY

Arriving

Travel documents: all visitors to the Soviet Union must have a visa as well as a passport. British citizens must possess a five or 10 year passport—a British Visitors' Passport is not acceptable. Passports should be valid for at least three months after returning from the Soviet Union. Visa applications must be made two months and not later than three weeks before departure. Visa applications will not be accepted after 14 working days before departure. Your travel agent will advise you on how to apply for your visa or can make the application for you. If you apply direct to the Soviet Consulate you will need a letter from a travel agent confirming your travel arrangements.

By air: the easiest way to get to Moscow and Leningrad is to fly. There are several direct flights daily from London to Moscow, leaving from Heathrow and Gatwick, one weekly flight from Manchester and a service from Glasgow. There is also a weekly flight from London to Leningrad. Pan-Am operates three weekly non-stop flights between New York and Moscow, with connecting services over London and Frankfurt. Aeroflot operates five weekly flights from New York to Moscow.

Most international passengers to Moscow arrive nowadays at the modern Sheremetyevo-2 airport in Moscow. It is about 19 miles (30km) northwest of the city centre. Leningrad airport is at Pulkovo in the south of the city. Much the cheapest way to get to Moscow or Leningrad is on a package tour. Holidays to Moscow and/or Leningrad are currently being offered by Thomson, Intourist, Liberty/Travelscene, Page and Moy, Sovereign and Serena, and the list is growing all the time. These can be excellent value for money. Independent travel is vastly more expensive.

After you have passed through Health and Immigration control, your passport and part of your visa will be returned to you. Pick up your luggage and proceed through customs. This is a much less daunting experience than it used to be, but it still takes time (an hour is by no means unusual). A green channel has recently been introduced at Sheremetyevo-2 but does not yet appear to be fully operational.

Moscow Air Terminal, Leningradsky Prospekt 37 (tel: 155–5004/5; Metro Aeroport).

Leningrad Air Terminal, Nevsky Prospekt 9.

By rail to Moscow: there are two routes to choose from. The first, via Ostend, Aachen, Hannover, Berlin, Warsaw and Brest leaves from London's Victoria Station; the second, via the Hook of Holland, leaves from London Liverpool Street. The journey time is usually about two and a half days.

Train services operate in summer and winter but schedules vary. Sleeper-car reservations are obligatory on trains to Moscow and should be booked at least six weeks prior to departure.

By rail to Leningrad: there is a daily service from Paris, via Cologne, Hanover, Berlin and Warsaw.

By road: you will have to stick

A Russian traffic hazard: snow

precisely to a route laid down in advance by Intourist, who will also make the arrangements for accommodation or campsite location, payment for which must be made in advance in hard currency. Detours are forbidden. You will need a good working knowledge of Russian in order to follow road signs, buy petrol and, if necessary, cope with a breakdown. Not put off? Then see **Driving**, page 113.

By boat: it is possible to reach Leningrad by sea from Britain. The Baltic Steamship Line operates summer sailings from Tilbury and there is a car ferry all the year round from Stockholm. The same company runs a summer passenger service from Helsinki.

Camping

Site places must be booked in advance with Intourist. When you have done this and paid for your trip you will be issued with a 'camping pass', which confirms the booking and which must be included with your visa application. Moscow's camping site is at 165 Mozhaisky Shosse, 10 miles (16km) west of the city (tel: 446 5141); open 1 June to 1 September. The overnight charge includes the cost of electricity, cooking facilities, kitchen utensils and tableware, as well as the use of sanitary and laundry facilities. It is possible to hire camping equipment in the Soviet Union but, to be on the safe side, take your own—there may be shortages. The same applies to food—take as much as you can with you.

DIRECTORY

The nearest campsite to Leningrad is 30 miles (48km) away at Repino (tel: 231 6839).

Chemist see Pharmacist

Crime

Generally speaking, the streets of Moscow and Leningrad are much safer than most major Western cities. There are relatively few cases of muggings and you can travel alone on the Metro in safety, even late at night. If you are the victim of a crime, you should inform your Intourist or travel representative immediately, then your embassy. You will also need to report the loss to the police. Make sure you have an

The cold has its compensations for Russia's younger generation

interpreter from Intourist or a fluent Russian speaker with you. If you lose money and/or your currency declaration form you will be unable to exchange hard currency for roubles without a written authorisation known in Russian as a *spravka* (certificate). Do not leave the police station without this. If you need to call home, your embassy may allow you to call direct; otherwise, you will have to book a call at your hotel

Avoid the following: foreign currency speculation; smuggling documents or packages out of the Soviet Union on someone else's behalf; any dealings in or use of drugs; jay walking (use the underpasses and observe the red lights. If you hear a policeman's whistle, stop and signal that you have understood. To ignore him will mean getting a public lecture in front of your friends and passers by).

Customs Regulations

All foreign currency in travellers' cheques and banknotes, and all valuables (including watches, medals, rings) taken into the Soviet Union, must be declared on a Customs Declaration Form. Keep this safe—you will need it to change money and it must be handed over at the airport prior to departure.

You can bring any amount of foreign currency into the Soviet Union, but not roubles. You must not bring in letters, messages, money, etc on behalf of third parties without official permission. Narcotics of any kind are absolutely prohibited, as is pornography. You may not bring in 'anti-Soviet' literature but Western novels are permitted.

You may bring into the country 250 cigarettes or 250 g of tobacco, a litre of spirits and 2 litres of wine, perfume for personal use, two watches, two still and one movie cameras, a radio, a portable typewriter, 100 grams of tea, 250 grams of coffee, a musical instrument, sports equipment, personal effects (including a bible) and a reasonable quantity of foodstuffs and gifts up to a value of 30 roubles.

Visitors may take out souvenirs and personal effects. In the case of furs, cameras and jewellery bought in the Soviet Union, the receipt must be produced. Antiques and *objets d'art* may be taken out only with a permit from the Ministry of Culture and on payment of a duty of 100 per cent of the value of the articles as shown in the permit.

On departure, you will fill out another declaration form, the details of which will be compared with those on the original form.

Driving

You will need an international driving licence or a national licence, which must have an insert in Russian, the booklet *Instructions for Foreign Motorists* (issued by Intourist prior to departure) and petrol vouchers (*Talon*) and a certificate promising to take the car back out of the country (to be registered with customs at the point of entry).

If you intend driving your own car, take out a short-term insurance policy to cover accidents, damage and third-party liability with the Soviet insurance organisation, *Ingosstrakh* (contact Intourist for details). Ingosstrakh insists on its coverage in many cases, even if this duplicates foreign insurance. Remember that you are not allowed to leave the confines of Moscow without informing Intourist first. Traffic in the Soviet Union travels on the right. The speed limit is 37mph (60kph) in central Moscow and 50mph (80kph) on the outer roads, but watch out for special lanes reserved for 'official' cars. Traffic coming from the right has right of way. Trams and buses have priority over other vehicles. If a tram stops to pick up passengers, you must wait for it to move off again before overtaking.

Parking: you can park almost anywhere, within reason. The 'No Parking' sign is a blue circle with diagonal red cross.

Theft: there is much less chance of your car being stolen or tampered with in the Soviet Union than in the West, but don't tempt providence. Many Russians moonlight as mechanics and you may well find hub caps and wing mirrors disappearing if you're not careful. Make sure your car is locked at all times and follow Intourist's advice about where to park overnight. Ask Intourist for addresses of petrol stations and for the necessary vouchers. The current cost of petrol is about 2 roubles a gallon (4.5 litres).

Accident or breakdown: contact the Intourist service bureau or the nearest Intourist service desk.

Remember: in the Soviet Union it is an offence to drive after consuming *any* alcohol.

Car hire: public transport in both Moscow and Leningrad is so cheap and efficient that it really is not worth hiring a car just to ride around town. If you want to hire a car for an excursion, see Intourist. Hiring a car costs 24 roubles a day, plus 10 kopeks for each kilometre you drive. The hire cost includes insurance for third party liability and servicing. For full insurance, protecting you against the cost of repairs, however, you must pay

an additional 1.5 roubles per day. Nissan of Japan now operate a car hire service jointly with Intourist from Leningrad (contact the desk at the Hotel Leningrad). You can opt either for self drive or a chauffeur service. Models available include Urvan, Microbus (10-seater), Sunny and Bluebird. Rates vary according to model from 24–78 roubles. Minimum period of hire is one day for self drive or three hours with chauffeur. Petrol rate is not included in self drive charge. The charge for self drive insurance is 2 roubles per day.

Electricity
The standard current in the Soviet Union is 220 volts. For power sockets you will need a plug or an adaptor with circular pins. Use of a hair dryer is forbidden in Soviet hotels. Avoid using too many appliances at once or you may find you have fused the circuit.

Embassies and Consulates
Australia: 13 Kropotkinsky Pereulok (tel: 246 5001)
Canada: 23 Starokonyushenny Pereulok (tel: 241 5882)
UK: 72 Naberezhnaya Morisa Thoreza (tel: 231 8511)
US: 19/23 Ulitsa Tchaikovskogo (tel: 252 2451)
The US Consulate-General in Leningrad is at Ulitsa Petra Lavrova 15 (tel: 274 8689)

Emergency Telephone Numbers
Fire 01, police 02, medical assistance 03

Entertainment Information
Available from Intourist. There is an Intourist desk in every large hotel which caters for foreigners.

To gain access to a hotel which is not your own, simply tell the porter 'Intourist' as you go in (you may not even be asked). The Intourist staff speak English, as well as other foreign languages. The **Moscow Excursion Bureau of Intourist** is located at 3–5 Ulitsa Gorkovo (tel: 203 4008).

Entry Formalities see Arriving

Health Regulations
Check with your travel agent before you book your holiday or buy your ticket. Alternatively, contact your nearest Intourist office (see **Tourist Offices**, below, for locations).
Free medical treatment is available to tourists on production of a passport, driving licence or medical card from home; some dental treatment is also free. The hotel should be able to call a doctor on your behalf.
Health precautions: do not drink the tap water in Leningrad. Use mineral water to clean your teeth and do not take ice with your drinks.
If you are unlucky enough to fall ill while on holiday, inform your hotel desk immediately. Medical care is free but if you are prescribed any drugs, you will have to pay for them. Western visitors get special treatment in Soviet hospitals, so if you have broken a bone or sustained some other minor injury, there is no need to worry—you will certainly be well looked after.
Casualty department: Sklifosovsky Institute, Sadovaya Ring near Kolkhoznaya Ploshchad (Metro: Prospekt Mira).

Entertainment can range from Russian folk songs performed on the balalaika *to the best of cosmopolitan culture*

Holidays

The following days are annual public holidays in the Soviet Union:

1 January (New Year's Day)
8 March (International Women's Day)
1–2 May (International Labour Day)
9 May (Victory in Europe Day)
7 October (Constitution Day)
7–8 November (Anniversary of October Revolution)

On public holidays museums and shops (except food shops) are closed.

Independent Travel

You are free to roam anywhere within the city limits. However, if you wish to go further afield, you must notify Intourist in advance.

Lost Property

If you lose anything, tell your tour representative immediately, or report the loss to the Intourist information desk in your hotel.

Media

Most major Western newspapers are on sale at hotel kiosks but supplies rapidly run

Spasskaya Tower in Red Square

out. The only foreign newspapers sold at street kiosks are the mouthpieces of the various foreign Communist Parties (eg, *Morning Star, L'Humanité, Avanti*).

If you take a short-wave radio with you, you should be able to pick up the BBC World Service on or around the following frequencies: 15070 kHz on 19-metre band; 12095 on 25 metres; 9410 kHz on 31 metres. Voice of America can sometimes be found on 9760 kHz on 31 metres; or try 6040 kHz on 49 metres. There will probably be a radio in your hotel room and television will certainly be available. Even if you do not know Russian, try a small dose of the Soviet media, just for the experience. Radio Moscow often has record request programmes, with a decidedly Russian flavour. On the hour, you will hear the distinctive time signal, followed by the bells of the Kremlin's Spasskaya, or Saviour, Tower. Soviet television has recently been given a big shake-up by its new head, Boris Aksionov (a former KGB officer). As a result, you can now see breakfast TV, late-night talk shows and incisive documentaries on controversial social problems like youth alienation and the drug culture, as well as the more traditional fare of ballet, drama, opera, film, etc. The evening news, *Vremya* (Time), goes out at 21.00 hrs.

Money Matters

The Soviet unit of currency is the rouble. One rouble = 100 kopeks. Coins are in denominations of 1, 2, 3, 5, 10, 15, 20 and 50 kopeks and one rouble.

Notes are for 1, 3, 5, 10, 25, 50 and 100 roubles.

The exchange rate fluctuates but at the time of writing is 10 roubles = £1 or $US1.56, following the devaluation of November 1989. Certain services however (especially in hotels), still operate on the old, pre-devaluation exchange rate. Items purchased at Beriozka shops (see pages 89 and 91), theatre and concert tickets, excursions, etc must be paid for in hard currency. Pay only with roubles in restaurants though you might like to tip in hard currency. Your hotel will have a 'currency bar', taking only foreign currency.

Take a variety of smaller denomination notes and coins with you, as a little now goes a long way. Take travellers' cheques issued by one of the major Western banks, and on no account take Eurocheques, which are still not commonly accepted. When you change money, you will receive a currency exchange receipt. Hang on to this and you will be able to change any left-over roubles back into your own currency at the airport before departure.

Credit cards: if you have one, it is probably worth taking it with you, as this facility is now gaining wider acceptance. You can even use your card in some restaurants, but check with Intourist first to avoid embarrassment! (Established credit cards—Visa and American Express, for example—can be used to obtain roubles, but bear in mind that

DIRECTORY

roubles acquired in this way cannot be converted back into hard currency prior to departure.)

The **American Express** office in Moscow is at 21A Sadovo-Kudrinskaya (tel: 254 2111/4495).

Opening Times

Shops generally open from 09.00 or 10.00 hrs to 20.00 or 21.00 hrs, Monday to Saturday, with a break of an hour for lunch (the timing of the lunch hour varies). Most food stores also open on Sundays. Beriozkas are open from 10.00 to 14.00 hrs and from 15.00 to 19.00 hrs on weekdays. Saturday closing is at 18.00 hrs; some open on Sunday. The **What to See** section gives times for individual museums, but check with Intourist before you set out. All museums are open on Sundays. Banks in tourist areas open from 08.00 or 09.00 to 20.00 or 21.00 hrs; some open round the clock.

Pharmacist

For the address of the nearest pharmacy (*apteka*), ask at the Intourist desk in your hotel. If you are on medication, make sure you take a full supply of the required drugs/preparations with you, as you are unlikely to obtain them in the Soviet Union. You will also need your own supply of contraceptives, tampons or sanitary towels, aspirin, diarrhoea tablets, antiseptic, plasters and perhaps a small roll of bandaging—and anything else you can think of! If you are visiting Leningrad during the summer months, you will need some form of anti-mosquito repellent. If you have a baby or small child with you,

take your own supply of nappies. Bear in mind that none of these everyday items is readily available in the Soviet Union.

Photographs

As you are no doubt aware, the Soviet authorities are extremely security conscious. You will not, then, be surprised to learn that you are not allowed to photograph or film the following: military and industrial installations, naval port facilities, research institutes, airports, railway stations, bridges, radio stations. Nor must you take photographs from the plane while flying over Soviet territory. More disappointingly, flash photography is often forbidden in churches and cathedrals, though you may sometimes get special permission (consult Intourist about this). If you break any of these rules (and some tourists do succumb to temptation) you risk having your film confiscated.

Soviet film is scarce and of poor quality, so bring a plentiful supply from home.

Places of Worship

Moscow Orthodox: Church of the Resurrection, Nezhdanovoy Ulitsa, 15 (Metro—Pushkinskaya).
Our Lady of Tikhvin, Tserkovnaya Gorka Ulitsa, 26a. (Metro—VDNKh).
St Nicholas in Khamovnikakh (the Weavers' Church), Timura Frunze Ulitsa, 1 (Metro—Park Kultury).
Holy Trinity, Vorobyevskoye Shosse, 3 (Metro—Leninskye Gory).
Baptist: Malyy Vuzovskiy

Leningrad's Church of St Nicholas

Pereulok, 3 (Metro—Ploshchad Nogina).
Mosque: Vypolzov Pereulok, 7 (Metro—Prospekt Mira).
Protestant: services are held at the British and American Embassies; phone for details (see **Embassies**, page 114).
Roman Catholic: St Louis, Lubyanka Malaya Ulitsa, 12 (Metro—Dzerzhinskaya).
Synagogue: Arkhipova Ulitsa, 8 (Metro—Ploshchad Nogina).

Leningrad Orthodox:
St Nicholas, Ploshchad Kommunarov, 13.
Trinity Cathedral, Ploshchad Aleksandra Nevskogo (Metro—Ploshchad Aleksandra Nevskogo)
Baptist: Bolshaya Ozornaya, 29a
Mosque: Prospekt Maksima Gorkovo, 7 (Metro—Gorkovskaya)
Roman Catholic: Kovensky Pereulok, 7 (Metro—Ploshchad Vosstaniya)
Synagogue: Lermontovsky Prospekt, 2

Police
The emergency police telephone number is 02. See

DIRECTORY

Crime, page 112.

Post Office

Every Intourist hotel has its own post office counter where you can buy postcards, stamps and envelopes (newspaper kiosks also sell stamps). There will also be a post box in your hotel and you can send telegrams from here.

Moscow: English is spoken at the international post office at Komsomolskaya Ploshchad, 10 (tel: 294 7555). Open from 09.00 to 20.00 hrs.

The Central Telegraph Office is located at Ulitsa Gorkogo, 7 (24 hour service; tel: 294 4750). International telephone calls can also be made from here.

Poste restante (*Do Vostrebovaniya*): mail should be addressed c/o Intourist, Moscow

The Leningrad Metro

K600 (the address of the Intourist Hotel on Ulitsa Gorkogo, 3, where mail can be collected).
Leningrad: Central Post Office, Ulitsa Soyuza Svyazi, 9, (tel: 06) open 09.00 to 21.00 hrs.
Central Telegraph Office: Ulitsa Soyuza Svyazi 14 (24-hour service). Poste restante: Nevsky Prospect 6, Leningrad C400.

Public Transport

Metro: Moscow and Leningrad both have cheap, clean, safe and efficient Metro systems and you will certainly want to use them. However, a basic knowledge of the cyrillic alphabet is well-nigh indispensable if you are to avoid getting lost, so it is worth investing the small amount of time necessary to master it before you embark on your holiday (See **Language**, page 125).

Before you set out, note down the cyrillic form of the station you are heading for, together with the names of any stations where you have to change lines. If you get lost you can ask someone to help you of course, but this is not easy during rush hours (roughly 06.30–09.30 hrs and 16.30–19.00 hrs). You will be less likely to panic if you have a friend with you, so avoid travelling alone if you can possibly help it.
Stations are indicated by a large red neon letter **M**. There is a flat fare of just 5 kopeks, irrespective of the distance you are travelling or the number of changes you intend to make. You pay again only if you break your journey by passing through the exit barrier. If you do not have any change there are machines at each station which give out 5 kopek

coins for 10, 15 and 20 kopek pieces. You can change rouble notes at the window marked касса)
The escalators are usually deep (especially in Leningrad) so if you suffer from vertigo, hold on tight to the handrail! Note, too, the absence of advertisements. Once you arrive on the platform you can expect a train within three minutes, even outside the rush hours. The illuminated clock at the end of the platform tells you how long it is since the departure of the last train.
As the carriage doors are about to close, a loudspeaker inside the train will announce:
Ostorozhna, dveri zakrivaetsya, sleduyushaya stantsiya...
('Attention, the doors are closing, the next station will be...') You will usually be able to find a seat. If you are young and able-bodied, however, be prepared to stand for an elderly person, as you will find many Muscovites doing in a crowded train (simply point to your seat and say *Pazhalsta*). As the train pulls into the next station its name will be announced, followed by any information about changing lines. So if you listen carefully and keep an eye on the map, you will be able to check whether you are going in the right direction or not. Changing lines takes time and can be tricky.
To know which direction to go in, look for a sign with the word *perekhot* (переход) and the name of the station you want. To get to street level, look for the sign *vykhod* (выход).
Basic signs:
entrance вход
exit выход

DIRECTORY

no entry   нет входа
cash desk   касса
to trains for stations...
к поездам до станчий
change trains for stations...
переход на поезда до станчий
exit for the town   выход в город
to the exit   к выходу

The Metros of both cities are open from 06.00 to 01.00 hrs sharp. (Take note: you will not be able to change lines after that time.)

Buses, trams and trolleybuses: trams are commonplace in Leningrad but not so common nowadays in Moscow. You will find buses and trolleybuses in both cities. All these forms of transport tend to be rather uncomfortable and crowded but you might like to take a ride just for the experience. The fare is the same as the Metro: 5 kopeks. Either buy your ticket from the driver or get on with your 5 kopek coin at the ready. Punch your ticket in the same manner as the other passengers or drop your coin into the box near the driver or at the back of the vehicle. If you can not get through, pass your money to a neighbour and say *Piridayite, pazhalsta* ('Pass it on please'). You will eventually be given a white paper ticket in return. As you see your stop approaching, say, *Vy seychas vihoditye?* ('Are you getting off now?').

Taxis: You can ask the Intourist desk at your hotel to book a taxi for you, but make sure you order it at least an hour in advance. All taxis carry meters and what they show will be the fare. Do not be surprised if the driver picks up another passenger. It is to your benefit, because if they are going in your direction the fare is shared. Your driver will certainly expect a tip and will be delighted if this comes in the form of a packet of Western cigarettes or a *little* hard currency.

Calling a cab on your own behalf is a little more tricky. The city cabs are yellow, with a chequered band on the sides or roof. A taxi stand is marked with the letter **T**. If you pick up a taxi from outside your hotel, be prepared to pay for the privilege, and in hard currency. A green light in the corner of the windscreen indicates that a taxi is for hire. The chances are that there will not be a yellow cab in sight but, fortunately, you are not restricted to this comparatively rare bird. You will find hundreds of Muscovites using their private cars as unofficial taxis and, providing you agree on the fare in advance, it is perfectly safe to accept a ride in this way. Always make sure you have your destination written out clearly in cyrillic letters so that there can be no misunderstanding.
There are also minibus taxis which follow a fixed route between main-line stations and other important destinations. They run between 09.00 and 21.00 hrs.

Student and Youth Travel

Youth exchanges are organised by an offshoot of Intourist called **Sputnik**.
Moscow: International Youth Tourist Bureau, Lebiazhy 4, Moscow G19.
US: Council on International Educational Exchange, 205 East 42 Street, New York, NY 10017.

You may prefer to use the hotel phone, rather than queue for a booth

Canada: Canadian Federation of Students-Services, 187 College Street, Toronto, Ontario M5T 1P7.
You can also write to the following:
UK: East Europe Interchange, 186 Streatham High Road, London SW16 1BB
US: Institute of International Education, 809 United Nations Plaza, New York, NY 10017.

Telephones
Local calls from your hotel room are free. Long distance calls can be made from the main exchanges at Ulitsa Gorkogo 7 (Moscow) and Ulitsa Soyuza Svyazi 14 (Leningrad), where you pay in advance. Listen for the tone and then dial. Expect the local operators to speak only Russian.
Unless you have relatives or friends in the Soviet Union, you will probably not need to make a local call; and, if you do, you can always ask an Intourist representative to help you with the procedure.
International calls must be booked either through the service desk at your hotel, or with the floor attendant (*dezhurnaya*). You may have to wait up to 24 hours for your call to come through if the lines are busy.

Time
Moscow and Leningrad are three hours ahead of London and eight hours ahead of Washington and New York; seven hours behind Sydney; and nine hours behind New Zealand. Summer time (when local time is one hour in advance of the rest of the year) is from April until the end of September.

Tipping
Officially it does not exist but actually tips are expected from Western tourists in certain situations. In restaurants leave a

foreign currency tip (service and other charges are always included). Taxi drivers too will appreciate a small tip in foreign currency. Hotel staff, such as the maid and the *dezhurnaya*, will welcome a small gift of perfume, talcum powder or cigarettes. Similarly your Intourist guide, but do not offer money.

Toilets

Soviet public toilets are noxious, unpleasant and unhygienic, so use the facilities in hotels as far as possible. If you do need to use a public convenience you will have to depend on your own supply of toilet paper or tissues. There are 'superloos' at the Paveletsky Station in Moscow and on Leningrad's Nevsky Prospekt. There are also conveniences at main line stations and at most of the major tourist attractions. The nearest public toilet to Red Square is in the basement of GUM or by the Kutafya Tower.

Tourist Offices

Intourist Moscow: Prospekt Marksa, 16, Moscow 103009 tel: general 292 2260; UK dept 292 2697; US dept 292 2386; Excursions 253 2262
Canada: 1801 McGill College Avenue, Montreal, Quebec
UK: Intourist House, Meridian Gate, Marsh Wall, London E14 ; 71 Deansgate, Manchester M3 2BW; and 26 St Vincent Place, Glasgow G1 2DT
US: 630 5th Avenue, Suite 868, New York, NY 10111

A Leningrad ice cream stall

LANGUAGE

A few hours spent mastering the Russian alphabet before you go will be amply rewarded. Being able to decipher street names, metro stations, etc, will give you the freedom to wander around by yourself, rather than being shepherded in a group.

The interior of the dome of St Isaac's Cathedral in Leningrad

ul words and phrases

	zdrávstvuytye	здравствуйте
bye	dasvidániya	до свидания
morning	dóbraya útra	доброе утро
evening	dóbry viécher	добрый вечер
night	spakóyni nóchi	спокойной ночи
e/you're	pazhálsta	пожалуйста
lcome		
you	spasíba	спасибо
	da	да
	niét	нет
se me	izvinítye	извините
e?	gdyé?	где?
?	kagdá?	когда?
many?	skólka	сколько
much	skólka	сколько
	ya	Я
	my	мы
	naliéva	налево
	napráva	направо
ht on	pryáma	прямо
t speak Russian	ya nye gavaryú pa-rússki	Я не говорю по-русски
ou speak English?	vy gavarítye pa-anglíyski?	вы говорите по-антлцийски?
down please	napishíte eta, pazhálsta.	напишите это, пожалуйста

LANGUAGE

Alphabet

А	ah
Б	b
В	v
Г	g
Д	d
Е	ye (yellow)
Ё	yaw
Ж	zh
З	z
И	ee
Й	i (boil)
К	k
Л	l
М	m
Н	n
О	o (not)
П	o
Р	r
С	s
Т	t
У	ooh
Ф	f
Х	ch (Loch)
Ц	ts
Ч	ch (chain)
Ш	sh
Щ	shch (Ashchurch)
Ъ	hard sign
Ы	i (sin)
Ь	soft sign
Э	ay
Ю	yooh
Я	yah

Signs

entrance	вход
exit	выход
no entrance	нет входа
free entrance	вход свободный
toilet	туалет
gentlemen	мужской
ladies	женский
stop	стой, стойте
go	идите
crossing	переход
closed	закрыто
open	открыто
cash desk	касса
reserved, occupied	занято
vacant	свободно
no smoking	нельзя курить!
push	толкайте
pull	тяните
information	справочное бюро
restaurant	ресторан
lift	лифт
telephone	телефон
taxi	такси
street	улица
buffet	буфет
bar	бар
museum	музей
theatre	театр
books	книги
record shop (Melodiya)	мелодия
chemist	Аптека

INDEX

INDEX/ACKNOWLEDGEMENTS

The Automobile Association would like to thank the following photographers & libraries for their assistance in the preparation of this book:

J ALLAN CASH PHOTO LIBRARY Cover: St Basil's Cathedral, 9 Moskva River, 16 University, 35 Bolshoi Theatre, 38 Tsar Cannon, 50 Tomb of Peter the Great, 56 Hermitage, 59 Winter Palace, 92 Market Place, 93 Cosmos Hotel, 97 State Circus Poster, 98 Kirov Theatre, 111 Petrol Station.

P CORY 31 Alexander Gardens.

NATURE PHOTOGRAPHERS LTD 75 Hooded Crow (A J Cleave), 77 Saiga Antelope 78 Taiga (B Burbidge), 81 European Bison (S C Bisserot).

SPECTRUM COLOUR LIBRARY 6 Buskers Arbat Street, 10 Kremlin, 13 Cathedral of the Dormition, 18 Underground, 23 Space & Aviation Exhibition, 32 Shop Windows, 55 Aurora, 65 Alexander Nevsky Monastery, 72 Smolny Convent, 84 Food & Drink Kiosk, 89 Russian Dolls, 91 Gum's Department Store, 94 Ukraine Hotel, 105 Souvenirs, 106 Harbour Ferry, 123 Telephone Booths, 124 Ice Cream Seller.

ZEFA PICTURE LIBRARY UK LTD 4 Moscow at night, 15 St Nicholas Church, 26/7 Navodevichy Convent, 41 Kremlin at night, 45 Historical Museum, 48 Zagorsk's Cathedral of Assumption, 49 Peter I, 52 Palace Square, 53 Decembrists' Square, 62 Peter & Paul Fortress, 69 Nevsky Prospekt, 74 Petrodvorets Palace, 87 Café, 101 Zagorsk, 103 River Moika, 109 Red Square, 116 Spasskaya's Tower, 119 St Nicholas Church, 120 Pushkin Station.

USSR PHOTO LIBRARY 20 Pushkin Museum of Fine Art, 28 Museum of Serf Art, 66 Pushkin, 83 Kolkhoz Market, 112 Mother & Child, 115 Balalaika Player, 126 St Isaacs'.

The authors would like to thank Gillian Richardson of Thomson (Moscow) and Mark Chapman, student at the Pushkin Institute, Moscow, for their help, and the staffs of Intourist, British Airways, British Rail and Pan Am for answering queries.